A book of famous Old New Orleans Recipes

Used in the South for more than 200 years

OVER 300 AUTHENTIC CREOLE RECIPES

"After a Shower" The Little Green Shutter Courtyard Royal Street N.O.

Home of the Free French Movement in New Orleans

Used by Good Cooks *for Something Different*

Famous Old New Orleans Recipes

Original Copyright 1935 by George Mayer

Published by
Tony Frederick
3722 Tamara Street
Abbeville, Louisiana 70510

Printed in the United States of America
TOOF COOKBOOK DIVISION

STARR ★ TOOF

670 South Cooper Street
Memphis, Tennessee 38104

FOREWORD

New Orleans, the culinary capital of America, has been famous for the excellence of its cooking for more than two centuries. Tourists and visitors from all over the world make it a point to visit New Orleans' famed restaurants and eating places and the Crescent City has long been a veritable Mecca for the gourmet and the epicure.

In this volume are printed (many of them for the first time) hundreds of the secret recipes that helped this historic city to establish its fame. Herein is revealed the method of preparing many of the dishes which have caused countless thousands to spread the fame of the Crescent City's cooking throughout the civilized world.

These recipes and cooking hints have been painstakingly culled from old files and extracted from the yellowed pages of many a Creole family's treasured recipe book. By using the ingredients specified and following the simple directions carefully, any cook of moderate experience and skill will have no difficulty in preparing a delectable meal in the true Southern tradition.

There are two primary causes of the truly distinctive flavor of New Orleans cookery. The first is the use of the French "roux" as the foundation of every meat and fish dish. The second is the liberal use of well cooked onions.

A "roux" is made by taking a heaping teaspoonful of pure lard and two rounded tablespoonsful of flour, putting them into an iron skillet (if one is handy) and cooking them, stirring all the time, until the mixture is light brown in color. Now put chopped onions (dry or green, depending upon the season) into your skillet and stir and fry this mixture until the onions begin to brown a little at the edges. At this point, put in your crabs or shrimp, if you are making a gumbo or stew. The entire method is more fully explained in each individual recipe on the following pages.

The best utensil for the New Orleans or "Créole" type of cookery is the iron skillet, known in some parts of the country as a deep iron frying pan or deep iron pot. This pot cooks best over a moderate heat and does not burn the "roux" or onions, as often happens when thinner utensils are utilized. It is a rule in French cooking to use a rather hot fire at first while frying the "roux" or onions but as soon as water is added the heat is turned down so that the mixture boils gently. This retains the essential flavor of the food instead of allowing it to go up in steam.

When cooking crabs, it is again necessary to cook very gently. Once water has been added, never allow the mixture to boil hard or the taste will be ruined.

Fresh onions should be used whenever possible, though dried onions are sometimes added to fresh ones. Small quantities of parsley are used and green peppers, known as "bell peppers" in the South, are popular. These peppers are not hot but add a piquant and distinctive aroma and taste to many dishes.

In cooking meats, New Orleans cooks brown them thoroughly, season them liberally and then cook them slowly. Fish and vegetables likewise should be seasoned before cooking so that the seasoning is absorbed and becomes a real part of the flavor of the dish. Never season your food after it is cooked.

When you add water, do so slowly. Don't drown your cooking all at once. A teacup every ten minutes, with frequent stirring, is the approved French method. French cooking requires less lard and by all means use fresh lard, or lard substitutes. Bacon grease, suet or old frying lard will ruin any dish.

Remember that if the printed recipes make too liberal a portion to suit your own individual requirements, you can adapt the recipe to your own needs simply by reducing all the ingredients in proportion.

If you find it impossible to obtain some of these ingredients in your own city, we recommend that you write to the Publisher: Tony Frederick, 3722 Tamara Street, Abbeville, Louisiana 70510 and outline your needs. He will be pleased to procure for you these Creole ingredients which are absolutely necessary if satisfactory results are to be obtained.

Leo. L. Mayer

A BOOK OF FAMOUS OLD
NEW ORLEANS RECIPES
USED IN THE SOUTH FOR
MORE THAN 200 YEARS

CREOLE COFFEE

It is necessary to have a French drip coffee pot and good New Orleans coffee.

Place 1½ cups dry coffee in top (the dripper). Have ready some boiling water, and pour every three or four minutes a tablespoonful at a time, on the coffee until you have about a pint of coffee. Never allow this coffee to boil at any time. Always heat in double boiler.

In some of the French restaurants of New Orleans, to every pint of hot coffee is added two tablespoons of dry cocoa or chocolate, carefully dissolved. This is a secret that is usually carefully guarded, and never given out willingly.

PLANTERS PUNCH (JAMAICA)

1 part lime juice
3 parts rum – Bacardi preferred
4 parts crushed ice

Mix all together and shake well, serve in chilled glasses with a red cherry in each.

This drink is a favorite in the British West Indies and Cuba.

MORNING PICK-UP

1 spoonful sugar
1 egg
½ jigger Bacardi rum
½ jigger of port wine
1 glass milk

Cracked ice, shake well, strain into Collins glass with a little grated nutmeg on top.

BLACKBERRY WINE (PLANTATION)

¼ teaspoon nutmeg
2 gallons dewberries or blackberries
2 gallons boiling water
½ yeast cake
3 pounds sugar

This wine must be made in a 5 gallon stone or pottery crock, and should be kept on the kitchen table in good light, where it can be stirred several times a day. Cover top with cheesecloth and tin cover. Wash berries, drain in colander and place in crock. Bring to boil 2 gallons water, then pour immediately on berries in crock. Add sugar and stir for 15 minutes. In 25 hours add half a yeast cake. Stir well, and taste. If sweet as very sweet lemonade, it does not require any more sugar for the present. Twice a day, stir mixture, and mash berries. Taste every day, and add 1 cup of extra sugar. On the tenth day mash berries through colander, then strain through cheesecloth. Wash crock, and return to it the strained liquid. Allow to stand for nine days more, but taste every day to make sure that the wine is no less sweet than it was in the beginning. Siphon off or dip off of the sediment, and put in large bottles. Once every two weeks, pour into other clean bottles, leaving the sediment. Be sure to keep sweet and in six months you will have a most delicious wine of high alcoholic content. Don't cork too tightly until the wine is mature or it will blow the cork out.

WHITE WINE (FRENCH RECIPE)

For making 5 gallons of wine use an 8-gallon crock or jar.
Boil 5 gallons of water and allow to cool.

14 boxes 12 oz. Del Monte seedless raisins or
11 boxes 15 oz. muscal Sun-Maid raisins (seedless)
8 pounds granulated sugar
5 pounds good grade rice
5 lemons, strain and use juice only
4 cakes of yeast

Dissolve the sugar in the 5 gallons of water, add the raw rice to it and mix well with wooden spoon. Chop the raisins fine in wooden bowl and add to mixture strained lemon juice, then add 4 yeast cakes dissolved in a cup of water. Mix well and let stand for 48 hours, then stir well again. Repeat this until fermentation stops, which will be in about 18 days. Strain off solid matter and bottle carefully. Examine often.

MOCK SHERRY

4 pounds seedless raisins
1 gallon boiling water
1½ pounds sugar
1 quart grape juice
½ yeast cake

Chop raisins fine in wooden bowl, put in crock with sugar and boiling water, add quart of grape juice and in 12 hours add yeast cake. Stir several times a day for 18 days, then draw off and strain as in recipe for blackberry wine.

GIGOLO COCKTAIL

To half quart of Bacardi add the peel of –
½ lemon, chopped fine
½ orange
½ apple with a part of pulp
½ mandarin
½ pint of Maraschino cherries
2 slices of pineapple, chopped fine

Add to above enough syrup, made of sugar, and water, boiled until thick, to fill quart bottle. Shake and let stand two weeks. Delicious when served with crushed ice.

HAPPY'S SPECIAL

½ teaspoon Herbsaint
1 dash bitters
1 jigger whiskey
1 teaspoon sugar
lemon peel
1 Maraschino cherry

Dissolve sugar thoroughly in small amount of water in water glass. Then add bitters, whiskey and cracked ice. Stir well. Get your cocktail glass and drop the lemon peel into it squeezing it well to extract the oils. Drop cherry, strain mixture into cocktail glass and serve.

The above for one cocktail. You may increase quantity proportionately for large numbers.

CHERRY BOUNCE

5 gallon glass bottle
(mineral water bottle)

Fill 5-gallon bottle to the very top with wild cherries, shake, then fill again to the top with more cherries. Of course you have washed the cherries before putting in bottle. Fill the bottle to the top with good grade whiskey. In 6 months pour off bounce, remove cherries from bottle, put back into bottle, add syrup of 2 pounds sugar, 1 cup boiling water.

CHERRY WINE

Proceed exactly as with blackberry wine. Procure from grocery a 2-gallon can of pie cherries. When the wine is 18 days old add 1 tablespoon best quality almond extract. Allow to mellow for 6 months.

WHITE WINE PUNCH

15 lemons, 12 for juice, slice 3 thin
6 oranges, juice
1 can shredded pineapple
1 cup gin
2 quarts white wine
1 quart water
2 pounds sugar
1 bottle, quart, red cherries.
   Do not use liquid.
1 can white cherries

Boil sugar and quart water 10 minutes. Mix in punch bowl or glass. Add next fruit, let stand 2 hours. Just before serving add wine and gin.

PEACH BRANDY

5 dozen very ripe peaches
4 pounds sugar
½ yeast cake
1 quart boiling water

Plunge peaches in boiling water, skin and cool and cut away all rotten spots, cut and put into glass receptacle or crock. Boil sugar and 1 quart water together for 5 minutes and pour immediately over peaches. Stir well in 24 hours, add yeast. Stir well twice a day. In 15 days strain fruit off, return to crock 15 days more, then strain, leave sediment in crock bottle. If not very sweet, add 1 pound sugar. Bottle again in 1 month, leaving sediment.

Drink in one year.

HOT EGG NOG

2 quarts milk
12 eggs
1 pound sugar
   quart whiskey

Beat yolks eggs to light color, add sugar, beat 10 minutes more, have milk heated to near boiling point, pour slowly the hot milk into egg mixture.

Beat white of eggs to stiff froth, and add whiskey, then top each glass with beaten egg white.

FRUIT PUNCH

Juice of 6 oranges, 12 lemons, 1 can each of shredded and sliced pineapple, 1 can white cherries, 1 large bottle Maraschino cherries, 1 gallon water, 4 or 5 cups sugar. Will serve twenty people. Ice just before serving.

HAPPY LIL

1   teaspoonful powdered sugar
2   ounces rum
2   ounces Hennessy's 3 star Cognac
    brandy

To the beaten yolk and white of egg (singly beaten) and added together, add water to fill glass and slowly but thoroughly mix all ingredients, and top with a dash of nutmeg. Serve in crushed ice.

THE KINGS COCKTAIL

½   jigger simple syrup
1   tablespoon Peychaud's bitters
1   tablespoonful Angostura bitters
3-4 drops of absinthe
½   ounce whiskey
½   ounce Italian vermouth
½   ounce benedictine

Mix thoroughly and strain off into cocktail glass with crushed ice, and serve with slice of orange, or cherry on glass' edge.

SOUTHERN FIZZ

juice of half a lemon
1   barspoon sugar
1   jigger Bacardi rum or gin

Shake with cracked ice, strain into fizz glass and fill with syphon.

ANIZETTE

3   lbs. sugar
2½ pts. water
1   pt. alcohol
½   teaspoon ani or almond extract

Let sugar and water stand until thoroughly melted, strain through linen, add alcohol and extract, bottle, shake and let stand.

PEP TEA

tea
4   oranges
3   lemons
    sugar to sweeten

Make good strong tea, and while hot, add 4 oranges, 3 lemons, and sweeten and let cool. Serve in glasses of cracked ice, and garnish with mint leaves.

JUNE BRIDE

⅓   orange or pineapple juice
⅔   Bacardi rum or whiskey
1   dash apricot brandy
    cracked ice

Shake well.

FLOATING PALACE

⅔ *whiskey or Bacardi rum*
⅓ *Italian vermouth*
1 *dash apricot brandy*
   cracked ice

Shake well.

GOLDEN DAWN

2 *measures sweet cream*
1 *measure honey*
3 *measures whiskey or gin*
   cracked ice

Shake well until velvety smooth. Serve immediately.

RAMOS GIN FIZZ

½ *teaspoon orange flower water*
½ *lemon juice*
½ *lime juice*
1 *teaspoon powdered sugar*
1 *egg white, beaten well*
½ *glass crushed ice*
2 *teaspoons rich cream*
1 *ounce seltzer water*
1 *jigger gin*

Mix in this order: Crushed ice, fruit juices, cream, orange flower water. Shake vigorously. Add beaten egg and shake until tired. Shake again.

CREOLE CAFE AU LAIT

For five people, take 2 cups black coffee, (see recipe) and 3 cups sweet milk. Put in saucepan and allow to come to a boil. Watch carefully to prevent boiling over. Serve instantly in large cups, with sugar.

MINT JULEP

mint leaves
teaspoon sugar
one jigger bourbon whiskey
one pony rum

Crush mint leaves in a bar glass with a teaspoon sugar and tablespoon water. Add one jigger of bourbon and one pony rum. Pour into a tall glass, fill with fine crushed ice. Place sprigs of mint on top.

DRY MARTINI

(Splendid as an appetizer before dinner)
1 *measure dry gin*
1 *measure French vermouth*
1 *dash orange bitters*
   cracked ice
1 *queen olive*

Stir the gin, vermouth and bitters in the cracked ice, strain in cocktail glass. Put olive on the toothpick, immerse and serve ice cold.

PINK ELEPHANT

1 dash absinthe or Herbsaint
1 dash orange bitters
1 dash Peychaud bitters
  small slice lemon with peel
1 jigger Italian vermouth
1 jigger best bourbon whiskey
1 teaspoon granulated sugar
1 teaspoon water
  crushed ice

Stir the gin, vermouth and bitters
in the cracked ice, strain in cocktail
glass. Put olive on the toothpick,
immerse and serve ice cold.

SAZERAC

⅓ teaspoon Pernod
1 teaspoon simple syrup
2 dashes bitters
2 ounces bourbon

Put Pernod into Old Fashioned
glass and revolve glass until it is
entirely coated. Add other ingredients. Stir well and serve chilled or on
the rocks. A twist of lemon peel may
be added.

SIDE CAR

2 tablespoons French Cointreau
3 tablespoons French Cognac juice
½ lemon
  cracked ice

Mix and shake well in mixer,
strain and serve cold.

SUMMER SNOW

1 cup milk sherbet
1 measure dry gin

Pour gin over sherbet and whip to
fluffy foam in mechanical beater or
shake to foamy cream in shaker. A
delightful summer "pick-up."

SOUTHERN
GENTLEMAN

½ Bacardi rum or whiskey
½ Vermouth chambery
1 dash grenadine
  cracked ice

Stir well. Twist orange peel on top.

MEATLESS VEGETABLE SOUP (FRENCH)

5-6 qts. water
1 bunch carrots (about 6)
3 turnips
4 pieces of celery
1 small cabbage leaf
4-5 young onions
2 white potatoes
1 heaping tablespoon flour
1 rounded tablespoon lard
3 sprigs parsley

Wash well, but do not peel any of your vegetables, except onions. Chop or cut well, all carrots, turnips, celery, cabbage leaf and potatoes, and put into a big pot with cold water, on a moderate flame. By the time the water has come to a boil, put an iron skillet on the fire, put lard in and flour, and cook until brown, add chopped onions, fry until edges begin to brown, and put in a cupful of the soup mixture, stir well until all lumps are gone. Then pour all this into your soup pot. Put salt to taste and cook slowly for 2½ hours.

This makes a delicious soup and quite as nourishing as if made with soup meat. If desired, the last hour, a handful of spaghetti or rice may be added.

CHICKEN OKRA GUMBO

Fry your chicken as in recipe for stewed chicken page 27, and when brown add chopped onion and sliced okra. Fry slowly for an hour, stirring every few minutes, then add slowly 4 quarts hot water, cook 1 hour more, taste to see if seasoned properly, then serve with heaping tablespoon of boiled rice.

CRAB GUMBO

Proceed exactly as with shrimp gumbo, after you have scalded, cleaned, and cut your crabs in half and cracked the large claws with the nut cracker. Caution must be taken in boiling crab gumbo. For some reason, the taste of crabs is ruined by rapid boiling. Use the filet powder as in shrimp and chicken gumbo, and serve with large portion of boiled rice to each soup plate. Some people add 3 or 4 whole cloves to the crab gumbo.

WHITE OR RED BEAN SOUP

1 cup red beans or white
2 hard-boiled eggs
½ cup chopped ham
1 gallon water
1 large onion or 6 shallots
1 thin slice garlic
1 cup claret or port wine
2 tablespoons salad oil
3 tablespoons of flour

Put beans and water to boil for one hour and a half. At this time beans will be soft enough to rub through a colander several times.

Pour soup liquid through mashed beans. Return the strained beans and liquid to pot. Make a brown roux with oil, flour, fry onions and garlic until onion browns on edges, mix in soup and cook for 30 minutes more. Have ready 1 slice lemon for each plate, and 1 heaping teaspoon chopped eggs. Add cup wine to soup and serve in large soup plates with corn bread sticks. Beans may be soaked overnight as in white bean soup, to shorten cooking period and less water need be added.

Add the small pieces of ham for flavoring if desired.

TURTLE SOUP

1 *pound turtle meat*
3 *even tablespoons lard or cooking oil*
3 *even tablespoons flour*
1 *large onion, chopped fine*
3 *quarts hot water*
1 *small pod garlic (section)*
2 *sprigs thyme, chopped*

Put lard in iron skillet, add turtle meat, and fry brown, add flour and stir into a brown roux, add chopped onions, garlic, cook till tender, add small can tomatoes and cook for 15 minutes, stirring constantly. Add now 3 quarts boiling water, 2 sprigs thyme, chopped, 2 cloves, pinch each of allspice and nutmeg, 2 sprigs chopped parsley, salt and dash of black pepper. When ready to serve add to each plate a tablespoon chopped hard-boiled egg, tablespoon sherry and 1 thin slice lemon. This soup is a favorite in New Orleans.

OKRA SHRIMP GUMBO

3 *pounds shrimp*
2 *pounds okra*
2 *medium-sized onions*
  half pod garlic
2 *tablespoons lard or oil*

This gumbo is used in summer, when okra is plentiful in New Orleans markets, and is made only with green fresh okra. It is very seldom that a New Orleans housewife will use canned okra. Put lard in large aluminum pot, fry sliced onion until brown around edges, add peeled shrimp and okra, sliced in rings one-eighth inch thick. Cook on low fire, stirring every few minutes, for 1 hour. When the okra is not sticking to the pot or spoon, usually after 1 hour's cooking, begin to add slowly 1 cup every few minutes 1 gallon of hot water. Cover and cook slowly for another hour. Taste to see if it is salty enough, then serve. Serve with heaping tablespoon boiled rice.

THRIFT GUMBO

Leftover chicken or fowl of any kind (including bones)
1 *onion*
1 *large ear garlic*
3 *stalks celery*
1 *lb. shrimp or*
2-4 *crabs or*
1 *dozen oysters or some of each*

Season to taste, red pepper, black pepper, salt. Make brown roux with butter or shortening, add chicken or fowl that has been cut into small pieces with onion, garlic, celery, season and fry thoroughly, then add 2 quarts water, and shrimp, oysters or crabs, or all three, the parsley and onion top and let boil slowly for 1 or 2 hours. When ready to serve, add gumbo filé 2 tablespoons and serve with rice cooked a la creole.

CHICKEN GUMBO FILÉ

Proceed exactly as with stewed chicken a la Creole, except that a gallon of water must be used. The filet powder, 2 tablespoons, is sprinkled into it while hot (off the fire) before it is served. This is a delicious dish, and is always, without exception, served with boiled rice, a large serving to each soup plate. Of course, the chicken is served right with the gumbo.

CORN SOUP

2　*tablespoons shortening or lard*
5　*ears of corn (cut from cob) or*
　　1 can of corn
1　*onion*
　　small portion of garlic
2　*ripe tomatoes, or 1 small can of*
　　tomatoes
2　*pounds of shrimp*

Drop the corn with the shortening in deep pot with the chopped onion, garlic, and season with salt and pepper to taste. After this is well fried, drop the shrimp and fry a little longer, then add 2 quarts of water and let cook slowly. serve with fresh crackers.

(Clean your shrimp well as outlined on page 23.)

Canned vacuum packed dried shrimp may be used.

CHICKEN SOUP (FRANCAISE)

1　*large old rooster*
3　*gallons cold water*
1　*large onion sliced or*
6　*sliced shallots*
4　*cups chopped celery*

Clean carefully large rooster, 4 to 7 pounds, and put in large preserving kettle with 3 gallons of water. Cook at a slow boil for about 5 hours, until the legs and wings can easily be pulled apart. Salt to taste after 2 hours' boiling. Put celery and chopped onion in at the same time you put your chicken. Turn fire off, let stand several hours until cool, then put in half gallon or quart jars until needed. This will keep 3 or 4 days in cold refrigerator. The French think that little can be done to improve the taste of chicken soup, so the celery and onion is the only seasoning. When cooked the liquid should be reduced 1/2 in volume, and should be considerably over a gallon of soup. This soup is excellent food for invalids and young children. Hot, it is at its best, but can be served jellied, cold.

OYSTER GUMBO

4　*dozen small oysters and liquid*
2　*large onions, or bunch shallots*
1/2　*cup salad oil*
2　*heaping tablespoons flour*
1 1/2　*quarts hot water*
2　*thin slices garlic*
1　*sprig each thyme, parsley, 1 bay*
　　leaf, minced fine

Put salad oil in pot, heat, add flour and make roux. When brown add onions, fry until onions brown at edges, add garlic, oyster juice, of which there should be at least a quart, then add other seasoning, with a dash of black pepper. Do not salt until ready to serve, as oysters usually require no salt. Now add the hot water, boil slowly for 15 minutes, add oysters, cook 5 minutes more, then stir slowly into gumbo after removing from fire, add 2 tablespoons filé powder. Serve immediately with a heaping tablespoon of well cooked rice.

Oyster gumbo can be prepared in a short while, and is an excellent dish to help out a dinner when unexpected company appear.

Shrimp gumbo can also be made same way and is delicious.

CRAB OKRA GUMBO

1 tablespoon of lard
1 dozen crabs
1 piece of ham, or veal stew,
   or both
1 small can of tomatoes
   (or 6 fresh ones)
1 quart of okra
   Chopped onion, green onion top,
   thyme, bay leaves, parsley, a leek,
   salt, pepper, drops of tabasco
   Rice

Cut the okra in small pieces (after it has been cleaned and steamed). Scald the crabs, pull off the legs, and clean the crabs well; then quarter them, saving the quartered pieces and the claws for use in the gumbo. Fry the okra in the lard with the ham and veal stew (if used). Add 2 quarts of water, and the crabs and resume the gentle cooking, for about an hour.

Note: Flour is usually not used in an okra gumbo.

You may use fewer crabs, and use shrimp with them, if you like.

LOBSTER GUMBO

1 can of lobster, or 1 fresh lobster
1 bell pepper
1 large onion
1 pod garlic
1 stalk celery
   parsley and green onions

Make roux, as for stews and other gumbos and add lobster meat and seasoning. Let fry, then gradually add one quart of hot water. Let simmer slowly. Serve with gumbo filé and rice.

POTATO SOUP A LA CREOLE

Peel and put three large potatoes in 1¹/₂ gallons of water. Boil slowly for half an hour, and while boiling, have ready two large or six green fresh onions, chopped. Put one tablespoon lard in iron skillet and heaping tablespoon flour, make roux brown, then add onions, cook a few minutes, then add two cups finely chopped celery. Cook ten minutes, stirring, then add two cups potato water, boil hard for ten minutes then put in large pot with potatoes and potato water. Mash potatoes, season well, cook one hour longer. When ready to serve, add one cup milk. Delicious and economical soup.

VEGETABLE "BEEF" SOUP

2 pounds brisket and soup bone
1 large onion
1 large soup bunch (vegetable)

Place meat into a large pot of cold water, and skim when it begins to boil, after skimmed, add the vegetable that has been cleaned, and cut into small pieces. Season, salt, and pepper, and let cook slowly until the meat is very tender. Half an hour before serving, small spaghettini, or cup of rice may be added. The meat may be served with soup, or made into hash or salad as in chicken salad or serve with Cocktail Sauce (page 44).

OYSTER SOUP A LA NEW ORLEANS

4 *dozen medium-sized oysters and juice*
3 *cups finely chopped celery*
1 *large chopped onion or preferably 6 finely cut shallots*
1 *even tablespoon salad oil*
1 *heaping tablespoon butter*
1 *tablespoon finely chopped parsley*
2 *heaping tablespoons flour*
3 *pints water*
2 *cups boiled milk*

Put your oil and butter in large iron skillet, then add flour, stir slowly over moderate fire until your roux is a rich brown, add chopped celery and onions, stir and cook until onions and celery are brown. This will take about 10 minutes, then add oysters and juice, and cook slowly for another 10 minutes. Have ready 3 pints of boiling water, add slowly, and cook for ½ hour more. Serve as soon as possible after this time, and pour into the pot containing the boiled milk. Taste just before serving, add a little black pepper and you will usually find that the salt in the oysters is sufficient. Add parsley, salt, this soup will serve eight.

CRAYFISH BISQUE (SOUP OR STEW)

10 *lbs. large crayfish*
1 *onion*
1 *pod garlic*
2 *bay leaves*
2 *stalks celery*
3 *slices stale bread (preferably French bread)*
  parsley, salt, black and cayenne pepper to taste

Wash crayfish thoroughly, have large container of boiling water into which drop crayfish, boil for about 5 minutes. Drain, cool and shell, keeping about 36 of the larger heads which have to be cleaned out and thoroughly washed.

Stuffing: Chop crayfish tails and together with seasoning put into pan with small quantity of hot shortening. Fry until well done, then add bread which has been soaked. Stir until well mixed, cool, then stuff heads. Each head should be dipped in flour and fried brown, this keeps stuffing in heads, add warm water in proportions to suit taste for soup, or for stew just enough for heavy gravy. Cook slowly for 15 to 20 minutes. This may be served with steamed rice.

OYSTERS ROCKEFELLER

Procure oysters on the half shell, wash them and drain them, and put them back on the shells. Place ice cream salt to the thickness of about one half inch on a platter and preheat, placing the oysters that are on the half shells on the hot salt and run them in the broiler for five minutes. Then cover with the following sauce and bread crumbs and bake in hot oven until brown. Serve hot.

Sauce for Oysters Rockefeller
1 cup oyster water
1 cup plain water
¼ bunch shallots
1 small sprig thyme
½ cup ground bread crumbs toasted and sifted
1 ounce Herbsaint
1 cup best butter
¼ bunch spinach
1 tablespoon Worcestershire sauce
2 small stalks green celery

Grind all the vegetables in the chopper. Put the water and the oyster liquor together, and let boil vigorously for about five minutes then add the ground vegetables and cook about twenty minutes or until it's to the consistency of a thick sauce.

Stir in the butter until melted and remove from fire, add the Herbsaint, pour sauce over oysters on the shell, sprinkle with bread crumbs. Return to hot oven for five minutes and serve piping hot on the platter in which you cooked them.

CRAB MEAT AU GRATIN

2 cups white sauce (page 20)
2 cups crab meat
1 pimento
1 green pepper
1 teaspoon chopped parsley
½ coffee spoon Worcestershire sauce
2 thin slices of lemon
1 cup grated cheese

Place in pudding dish the above. Sprinkle grated cheese after tasting to ascertain if the seasoning is sufficient, and bake for 30 minutes in moderate oven. New Orleans restaurants are deservedly famous for this dish.

SHALLOW-FRIED FILLET OF SOLE

6 thin fillets of flounder
1 cup tomato catsup
1 cup dry, fine bread crumbs
Shortening from frying
Parsley for garnishing
Salt and pepper to season

Dip each slice flounder into catsup, then into bread crumbs which have been mixed with salt and pepper to season. Cut flounder as nearly 4x2x¼-inch as possible without wasting it. Shallow-fry in hot shortening. 385° F., 1 inch deep in heavy frying pan, until golden brown. Drain on absorbent paper. Serve hot, garnished with parsley.

CRAB STEW

1 *dozen crabs*
8 *shallots or 2 onions*
3 *tablespoons salad oil*
2 *heaping tablespoons tomato paste*
3 *tablespoons flour*
1 *thin slice garlic*
1½ *quarts boiling water*

Clean and cut crabs in two. Crack claws with nutcracker so they can be pulled apart at table. Put in iron skillet oil and flour, make roux, brown well, add chopped onions, brown, add crabs, tomato paste, stir well 5 minutes, then season and add slowly every few minutes, a quart and a half of water. Boil very gently for one hour after this. If gravy is not thick enough when ready to serve, dissolve 3 teaspoons flour in water, and add to slowly boiling gravy. Taste for seasoning, and serve with rice or cornbread.

This gravy is delicious. A large aluminum pot should be used as soon as the frying stage is past. A quart of gravy can be made from a dozen crabs, so a large pot is needed, as the crabs take up much room in a pot.

STEAMED REDFISH WITH CREOLE SAUCE

1 *redfish (4-5 lb.)*
   Salt and pepper to season

Wash redfish and dry thoroughly. Sprinkle with salt and pepper and tie in cheesecloth; steam 45 minutes. Remove cheesecloth, place fish in center of hot platter and pour Creole sauce over. Place small boiled potatoes on both sides and buttered peas at both ends of platter. Garnish with parsley.

SHRIMP A LA CREOLE

4 *pounds lake shrimp*
4 *green bell peppers*
1 *can Italian tomato paste*
1 *bunch shallots, or 1 large onion*
½ *small pod garlic, sliced*
¾ *cup salad oil*
3 *heaping tablespoons flour*
   Salt and pepper to taste

Clean shrimp as per instructions on page 23 and boil for five minutes and drain. Use iron skillet. Make a roux with oil and flour. Brown well, add onions, brown slightly. Put in shrimp, salt and pepper. Stir around in roux and onions, until each shrimp is coated with the roux, and none of the roux and onions sticks to the skillet. At this point, add the can of tomato paste and green peppers. Stir around for 15 minutes on moderate flame. after all tomato paste is sticking to the shrimp, pour 1 cup hot water in bottom of skillet and turn the flame low. Let cook for 15 minutes more, then stir well and add slowly 3 or 4 cups hot water. If this method is used carefully, the rich gravy will cling to the shrimp, but if the ordinary stew method is used, the shrimp will appear naked, with no gravy sticking to them.

Taste to see if there is salt and pepper enough, and serve after 1 hour's cooking. This is a delicious dish and New Orleans is famous for it, but so often what is advertised as Shrimp a la Creole turns out to be only shrimp stew.

This somewhat complicated method is the only one by which Shrimp a la Creole can be successfully made. It is worthwhile to follow it carefully.

FRIED SOFT SHELL CRAB

Fried soft shell crab is one of the dishes for which New Orleans restaurants are famous. Served with tartar sauce they make a delicious luncheon or dinner dish. First remove the soft feelers or "dead men" you will find under each side of the shell, then take out the eyes, mouth and sand bag under the mouth. Wash well, soak in mixture made of 1 egg, cup milk, salt and pepper and a few slices of garlic. Dip them in flour, fry in deep fat for about 20 minutes until brown. Drain on paper and serve garnished with sliced lemon and minced parsley. Serve with tartar sauce.

BAKED RED SNAPPER

6-8 *pound red snapper*
2 *large onions or 8 shallots*
1 *large can No. 2 canned tomatoes*
3 *sprigs parsley*
1 *sprig thyme*
1 *bay leaf*
3 *cups soaked bread*
3 *cups chopped celery*
$^{1}/_{2}$ *cup lard*
1 *whole clove*
1 *whole clove garlic, chopped*

The red snapper is the pride of the New Orleans fish market, and an inspiration to all Creole cooks. In Creole cookery, fish and meat are never boiled before baking, so you take your fish, scale it and remove the "innards," and stuff it before you put it in the oven. Make your stuffing as follows: Chop 8 young onions and fry them in iron skillet until brown on edges, then add your 3 cups soaked and squeezed bread. Fry and chop and mix well together until done. 15 minutes is sufficient time for this. Season with salt and pepper, and set aside to cool. One-half cup of lard may seem excessive for the frying of this dressing, but it can't be done with less. Mix 1 teaspoon salt, $^{1}/_{2}$ teaspoon black pepper with 1 heaping tablespoon of lard, and rub the fish inside and out with the mixture. Stuff the fish, place in long pan, and bake for 30 minutes in hot oven, then remove from the stove, and pour in this gravy which you made while the fish was baking. Fry your onions, sliced garlic in $^{1}/_{2}$ cup oil or lard, add can tomatoes, 6 cups water, clove, parsley, bay leaf, 3 cups chopped celery. Put this gravy, well seasoned with salt and pepper, into the pan with the fish, return to the oven and bake for 30 minutes more. Serve with mashed potatoes, and white wine as a beverage.

OYSTER PIE

2 *dozen medium-sized oysters*
6-8 *shallots*
2 *tablespoons salad oil*
1 *heaping tablespoon flour*
no salt and a little black pepper

Make roux with oil and flour. Fry shallots till brown, put in oysters and oyster liquid. Cook for 30 minutes slowly. Set to cool. When cool, put into 2 pie plates lined with pie crust. Have upper crust thicker than lower, $^{1}/_{4}$ inch and bake pie in hot oven. This pie is a delicious luncheon dish.

STUFFED CRABS

1/2 cup salad oil
4 cups crab meat
2 cups soaked and squeezed bread
1 bunch shallots or 1 large red
*   onion*
2 cups crab gumbo
*   Salt and pepper*

It is best to make crab gumbo and stuff crabs on the same day, because the gumbo or soup from crabs adds to the success of the stuffed crabs. Some cooks take the crab claws and shells that the crab meat has been taken from, put them in a pot with 1 quart boiling water and use in the stuffed crab after an hour's boiling. It answers the same purpose as the gumbo. Put oil in iron skillet; fry onions to light brown. Put in crab meat, add a little salt and pepper, then the bread, then 2 cups of gumbo in the making or liquid from crab shells. Cook for 15 or 20 minutes, stirring all the time.

Place in cleaned crab shell, toasted bread crumbs on top, and bake 20 minutes before serving.

FRIED SHRIMP

Clean selected large shrimp and drop into boiling water for a few seconds, drain, and season thoroughly, and dip into beaten egg, and rolled into flour same as trout, and fry in deep boiling fat until brown. May also be served with tartar sauce or tomato catsup and lemon.

FRIED OYSTERS

Select medium to large oysters. Drain, roll, two at a time in very fine corn meal, and drop instantly into boiling oil of fine grade. They should brown in one minute. Lift and drain on brown paper and serve immediately with tomato catsup. Don't put too many in the oil at once. They will be soggy and greasy if crowded.

WHITE SAUCE

Melt 2 tablespoons butter in skillet. Add 3 tablespoons sifted flour, stirring constantly until light brown. Then slowly add milk to desired consistency. Season with salt, pepper and parsley to taste.

TUNA FISH LOAF

1 can tuna fish
2 tablespoons tomato paste
1 medium-sized stuffed olive
1/2 teaspoon celery salt
2 1/2 cups water
1 envelope Knox gelatin

Pinch black pepper and salt to taste, dissolve gelatin, 1 cup cold water. Put 2 1/2 cups water to boil with tomato paste, celery salt and salt and pepper for 10 minutes. Then mix with gelatin, tuna fish and olives. Put in china dish to harden in refrigerator. Serve on a lettuce leaf and top with heaping teaspoonful of mayonnaise.

This is a nice dish for Sunday night supper as it can be prepared the day before.

COURTBOUILLON OF REDFISH

When natives of Louisiana (Creole Louisiana) go fishing, they take a long iron skillet or iron pot. This is for the courtbouillon. In the party will be a man, it's usually a man who considers himself an expert cook if his only dish is courtbouillon. He catches a large redfish, cleans, scales and cuts it into slices across the backbone. The slices should be about 3 inches wide. Now for the gravy.

Make roux with ¹/₂ cup salad oil, cup of flour, fry brown, add 2 large sliced onions, brown around edges, add a large No. 3 can of tomatoes, cook 5 minutes then add immediately the following:

2 bay leaves, chopped fine
¹/₄ teaspoon allspice
1 heaping teaspoon parsley
4 green bell peppers, sliced in rings
4 young green shallots, chopped fine
1 whole clove spice, 1 clove garlic, sliced
1 water glass claret wine
1 water glass water, drop by drop salt, and black pepper
2 very thin slices lemon
1 teaspoon port wine

Add the sliced fish now, boil in gravy for 20 minutes, lifting each piece gently every few minutes to prevent burning. Serve with mashed or french fried potatoes.

CREOLE SAUCE

1 can tomato soup
¹/₂ cup water
4 tablespoons green pepper, chopped
2 tablespoons onion, chopped
6 stuffed olives, chopped
1/2 teaspoon salt
2 tablespoons oleomargarine

Cook all together about 15 minutes. Serve over steamed redfish.

"SHRIMP ARNAUD"

3 pounds fresh shrimp (shelled and boiled) see page 23 for preparing shrimp

Make dressing by thoroughly mixing the following ingredients in the order given:

2 tablespoons vinegar
4 tablespoons olive oil
1 tablespoon prepared Louisiana mustard
2 green onions with tops, minced
1 quarter of a stalk of celery, minced
Salt and pepper to taste

Mix shrimp in a bowl, thoroughly, with the dressing, and set in the ice box for about two hours. When ready to serve, again mix well. Arrange each portion with a slice of tomato, and surround with lettuce.

Mr. Arnaud says that the secret of this delicious salad is in thoroughly marinating the shrimp with the dressing; in this way the shrimp absorb the unique flavor of the sauce. So mix the shrimp with the dressing and set aside in the ice box for at least two hours before serving.

CRAWFISH OR SHRIMP ETOUFÉE

2-3 *pounds peeled crawfish tails*
¹/₄ *pound butter – little oil*
¹/₂ *cup chopped celery*
1 *cup chopped onions*
2 *pods garlic*
¹/₂ *cup chopped bell pepper*
2 *tablespoons crawfish fat*
   (optional)
2 *cups cold water*
2 *teaspoons flour*
¹/₄ *cup onion tops & parsley chopped*
   Salt, black pepper & red pepper
   to taste

Parboil shrimp in little water with a little liquid crab boil. Use this liquid instead of water in preparing shrimp.

Crawfish – season crawfish tails with salt and pepper and set aside. Melt butter in heavy pot. Add flour and stir until blended. Add onions, bell pepper, celery and garlic and cook until onions are wilted – stirring constantly. Add crawfish fat, 1¹/₂ cups water, crawfish tails or shrimp, salt and pepper and bring to boil and cook over slow heat for 30 minutes stirring occasionally. Add onion tops and parsley and cook another 10 minutes.

CRAWFISH SUPREME

1 *lb. crawfish tails*
1 *medium onion*
8 *tablespoons butter*
3 *tablespoons flour*
¹/₂ *teaspoon white pepper*
1 *teaspoon garlic salt*
¹/₂ *cup white wine*
2 *tablespoons tomato paste*
2 *tablespoons chopped parsley*
   Milk

Melt half of butter, add flour and cream until thickened, then add milk making a medium sauce. Sauté onion and crawfish in rest of butter until onions are clear. Add pepper, garlic salt and parsley. Blend with cream sauce. Add wine and tomato paste.

FILET OF TROUT

To the trout that has been cleaned, tenderloined and dried, add the seasoning, red pepper, black pepper, and salt, then dip into beaten egg, and into flour that has a small dash of baking powder, and drop into deep hot shortening, frying until brown. Serve with tartar sauce and french fried potatoes. Garnish with parsley and slices of lemon.

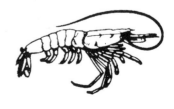

SALMON CROQUETTES

1 cup cooked salmon
1 tablespoon butter
1 tablespoon flour
1/4 cup milk or water
1 teaspoon lemon juice
1/2 teaspoon salt
1/8 teaspoon pepper

Make a roux with the butter, flour and milk. Put salmon into bowl and add the sauce, lemon juice and seasoning: mix with fork until salmon is well broken. Set aside and when cold, mold into desired shapes; roll in bread crumbs, then in egg beaten with 1 tablespoon cold milk, then in bread crumbs. Fry in deep hot fat at 385° F. until brown.

Prepare shrimp for cocktail as follows: First remove heads, shell and black in tails. This black will come out easily if shrimp are fresh. In all cases remove this even if you have to cut top of tail with a knife. Then wash tails and put in large pot cold water. Add 1 sliced lemon, half bell pepper, half onion, lots cayenne pepper and salt. A stalk of celery may also be added, then cook over fire boiling for at least 30 minutes. Remove from fire and let cool in same water, then drain and place shrimp tails on ice for cocktail or salad.

Never boil your gumbo after you have added the filé, *and be careful to sprinkle the filé slowly into the gumbo, stirring all the while. Added too fast, the filé will lump.*

EGG SANDWICH FILLING

3 hard-boiled eggs
2 cups mayonnaise
8 sweet pickles, sliced
15 stuffed olives
1/2 cup sweet vinegar from pickles
1/4 teaspoon each of salt and black
    pepper

Mash yolks of eggs up fine, add mayonnaise slowly, then sweet vinegar, then whites chopped very fine, olives and pickles, salt and pepper.

This makes a delicious spread for very thin sandwiches for afternoon tea or luncheon or picnics, as they keep for hours without deteriorating.

SCALLOPED EGGS WITH HAM

2 cups cold boiled ham chopped fine
4 hard-cooked eggs
1 cup cream sauce
2 cups bread crumbs
2 tablespoons milk

Cut eggs into slices; cover bottom of greased baking dish with 1/3 of bread crumbs; then add in layers eggs, ham, cream sauce and crumbs, having crumbs for top layer. Add milk and bake in moderate oven about 20 minutes.

RUM OMELET

Make plain omelet, serve on a plated silver dish, pour 1/2 cup rum over it, touch lighted match to it, serve immediately. Be sure the rum is of good quality, or it will not burn.

EGGS ANGELE

1 quart boiling water
18 hard-boiled eggs
2 envelopes gelatin
6 shallots, cut very fine
1 thin slice garlic

Use oblong pyrex pan for mould. Season well, salt and pepper.

Boil 6 shallots, garlic in 1 quart boiling water for 10 minutes, add gelatin, dissolve in 1/2 cup cold water.

Pour 1 cup of this liquid into dish used as mould, then cut eggs into round slices 1-3 inch thick until bottom is neatly covered. Pour a coating of liquid until eggs and liquid are all used up, then place on ice for several hours.

Turn upside down on platter arranged with lettuce leaves and decorated with stuffed olives and sweet pickles.

Serve at table as supper dish, slice with sharp knife. Put lettuce leaf, a pickle and olive on each plate, and top with teaspoonful mayonnaise.

SPANISH OMELET

1 cup canned tomatoes
2 green peppers
4 young onions
10 eggs
1/2 cup milk
1 tablespoon lard

Put lard and onions in skillet and fry slowly, add green peppers and tomatoes, fry 5 minutes more, then add egg beaten up with milk. Fry carefully until done and serve immediately.

EGGS WITH CREOLE SAUCE

12 hard-boiled eggs
3 tablespoons tomato paste
3 cups hot water
2 heaping teaspoons flour
2 tablespoons salad oil
2 green peppers
1 small onion or 6 shallots
1 thin slice garlic, salt and pepper

Set eggs to boil on very slow fire and never allow to boil hard, 15 minutes of boiling is enough. Put oil in iron skillet, stir in flour, brown, add cut onions and tomato paste, and stir for 10 minutes. Begin then to add water slowly; at this point pour this mixture into granite saucepan, add green peppers and garlic and rest of water and seasoning. Cook slowly for 30 minutes, then pour over halved eggs in deep dish. This is a delicious luncheon dish, served with hot biscuits and sweet potato croquettes.

EGGS FLORENTINE

1 bunch of boiled spinach
1 lump butter
2 eggs
   grated cheese

To chopped spinach add butter. Poach eggs, salt, pepper to taste. Make cream sauce. Put 1 tablespoon of butter in pyrex or earthenware dish, add spinach. Dress eggs over spinach, cover with cream sauce, and sprinkle grated cheese.

OYSTER OMELET

2 dozen oysters
1 heaping tablespoon butter
4 shallots
1 pod garlic
2 tablespoons minced bell pepper
2 tablespoons minced celery
2 bay leaves
   salt, bread, pepper to taste
4 eggs
2 tablespoons chopped parsley

Melt butter in saucepan and add minced garlic, bay leaves, pepper and celery. Drain the liquid from the oysters and put them into the butter with the seasoning, lower heat and let cook about 3 minutes. Beat the eggs together, add salt and pepper and turn them into saucepan with oyster mixture, but do not stir; when lightly browned turn onto hot platter, and garnish with chopped parsley.

SPINACH OMELET

1 lump butter
1 bunch spinach
4 eggs
   salt, pepper to taste

Clean and boil spinach, drain and chop. Beat eggs until light and fluffy, pour spinach into pot of melted butter, cook, then add beaten eggs, cook until done, serve piping hot.

STUFFED EGGS

Hard boil quantity of eggs desired, peel, cut in half, remove yolks and mash. Season yolks with chopped parsley, celery, salt, pepper to taste. Add olive oil, dash vinegar, and mayonnaise to make paste stuffing, stuff and shape, garnish with parsley and sliced stuffed olives.

(Minced ham and olives may be added to stuffing if desired.)

EGGS A LA CREOLE AND CHEESE

6 eggs
  salt, black and cayenne pepper
$^1/_2$ pint cream sauce
4 tablespoons grated cheese

Take a wide flat pyrex or casserole dish, butter it well, and pour in $^1/_2$ the sauce. Next, pour in the eggs that have been separately beaten (adding yolks to whites, mixing thoroughly. Pour some of eggs into casserole, sprinkle with grated cheese, then sauce alternately, until all is used up, the grated cheese should be on top. Bake in hot oven until eggs are done and the cheese melted.

CANAPÉ MARGUERY

$^1/_4$ pound tuna, chopped
1 ripe tomato, chopped
2 hard-boiled eggs, chopped
8 anchovies, chopped
$^1/_2$ green pepper, chopped
1 cup Russian dressing

Mix well and add dressing which is made as follows:

2 egg yolks
$^1/_4$ teaspoon sugar
1 teaspoon vinegar
1 teaspoon mustard
1 cup olive oil, mixed slowly
  salt and pepper to taste

Assemble the above and beat with egg beater, then add

1 large pimento, chopped
4 large olives, chopped
1 tablespoon catsup

The Russian dressing that has been added to the first mixture may be kept on ice for almost any length of time. Just before serving, put tablespoon butter in heavy frying pan, blend with tablespoon of Worcestershire sauce, mixing together and heating thoroughly. Serve immediately on hot toast made by frying in the butter and Worcestershire mixture or just plain toast. It is important to have it very hot. This can be made at the table as Crepe Suzette.

BEEF OR VEAL ROUND (A LA CREOLE)

For six people, take about 2 pounds of beef or veal round, trim off all tallow, and put in skillet with 3 tablespoons lard. Salt and pepper, and fry well until all water is cooked out of meat, and when it is brown, add 3 level tablespoons flour, stir until brown, add two medium sized dry onions, chopped fine, 1 can tomato paste, fry a few minutes more – then add gradually 2 cups water. Allow this to cook slowly, adding water until the iron skillet is almost full of water, then add, after an hour's cooking, 7 or 8 young green onions, chopped fine. This meat requires about 3 hours slow boiling in the gravy. Be sure to add water from time to time to keep the iron skillet almost full, turning the meat over every 15 minutes. This gravy is very delicious, and should always be served with boiled rice.

LIVER A LA CREOLE

1 *pound sliced beef or calf liver*
3 *tablespoons salad oil*
1 *large onion, sliced in rings, thick*
1 *green pepper*
1 *heaping tablespoon flour*
  Salt and black pepper

Put salad oil in iron skillet to get very hot. Put sliced liver in oil and fry rapidly for 10 minutes. Remove from skillet to plate, make roux with remaining oil and flour, brown well. Add onions, fry brown, put liver in with roux, then stir until liver is coated with roux, then add very slowly 2 cups hot water, season. Add green pepper cut in rings. Cook 10 minutes more, and serve. Entire cooking time $^3/_4$ hour. Serve at breakfast or supper with grits.

STEWED CHICKEN WITH RICE, SPAGHETTI OR NOODLES (a la Creole)

1 *half-grown chicken or hen (still young)*
1 *small can tomatoes*
2 *medium-sized onions (chopped fine)*
5 *young green onions (chopped fine)*
3 *even tablespoons lard*
4 *even tablespoons flour*

Have your chicken cut up and ready. Sprinkle well with salt and pepper. Put iron pot or frying pan on hot stove, and fry the chicken rather slowly for about half an hour, stirring every few minutes to keep from burning. When it is rather brown, put in flour, and stir until you have a brown "roux," then add the chopped dry onions, and fry until they brown at edges. Your green onions will go in later. Have a small pot of hot water on the stove, and add slowly, stirring, to the chicken, until you have used about a pint. Add your chopped green onions, taste to see if it is salty enough, add another pint of hot water slowly, taste again, and cook slowly, just boiling, for almost an hour. If the gravy cooks down too much, there should be about a pint when it is done, add more water. Serve with boiled rice and sweet potatoes cooked in any way.

Chicken gravy and rice make a very delicious dish, and stewed or baked chicken is always served with rice in the rice-eating parts of the South.

CHICKEN PIE A LA CREOLE

Use recipe for stewed chicken and recipe for biscuits. Line deep pudding pan with dough. Have ready stewed chicken, cold, very important, put in chicken and gravy, roll out top crust 1/3 inch thick, and bake in moderate oven 25 or 30 minutes. Grease pan well with lard. This recipe is Creole in origin and is seldom made anywhere but in southern Louisiana.

LIVER DELICIOUS

1 pound sliced veal liver
2 onions (chopped fine)
1 pod garlic
  Parsley and green onion tops

Remove thin skin of liver edges and slit to keep from curling up. Season thoroughly with salt, red and black pepper. Dip into flour, and drop each piece into hot lard frying quickly until browned. Add onion, garlic, parsley, green onion tops and a few drops of vinegar on each slice of liver. Cover and cook slowly until onions are done. A tablespoon of water will keep from sticking. Delicious when served with grits or mashed potatoes.

ROLLED ROAST OF BEEF

Ask dealer to prepare boneless, rolled roast from 5 to 6 pounds rib of beef. Sprinkle with salt and pepper, place in open roasting pan with shortening. Do not cover or add water. Roast in moderate 350° F. oven. Allow 22 to 25 minutes per pound for well-done meat.

BAKED BEEF ROUND

6 pound beef round
1 medium-sized onion
1 pod garlic
1/2 cup lard

Make small holes in beef round, and insert a piece of onion and a small piece of garlic in each one. After this is done be sure you have cut away all the tough pieces of string and gristle from outside of beef round. Mix lard with 1 teaspoon salt and 1/2 teaspoon of black pepper. Place in hot oven and bake for 45 minutes, then remove for 5 minutes from oven and pour over the roast gravy given below. After returning roast to oven use a moderate oven, and baste with gravy every 15 minutes. Serve dry in separate dish and serve gravy in gravy dish.

Make roux in iron skillet with 1 tablespoon lard, 2 tablespoons flour, 1 chopped onion, 2 tablespoons tomato paste, 1 green pepper and 1 quart hot water. Cook for 15 minutes in skillet then pour into roast pan, and bake as directed above. This roast is delicious cold.

Serve rice with this gravy.

Do not bake more than 1 hour after you add the gravy.

BROWN ROUX

2 tablespoons shortening
2 tablespoons flour

Heat shortening, add flour, stirring slowly until brown, salt and pepper to taste. This roux is the basis for most Creole cooking, and is adapted in various ways, serving as a base for grillards, gumbos, stews, etc.

STUFFED FOWL

After fowl (chicken, duck, goose or turkey) has been cleaned and DRIED it is dropped into roaster WITHOUT ANY SEASONING WHATSOEVER, into hot grease sufficient to keep it from sticking, then cover. Turn at intervals so as to brown. This is done ON TOP OF THE STOVE (not in the oven) over a slow fire. When thoroughly browned remove and season IN AND OUT with salt, cayenne and black pepper. If fowl is to be stuffed – stuffing is inserted at this time and fowl sewed. It is then put back into the same roaster and into the same grease, covered and placed in hot oven at about 350°. Baste at intervals until thoroughly done. If covered tightly water will not have to be added, but a small amount can be added if necessary.

Stuffing

Have giblet, livers and heart ground with one bell pepper, 1 stalk celery, 1 onion and small clove garlic. Season then drop into hot grease. Let brown cooking slowly and stirring almost constantly. Then add about 3 or 4 slices stale bread preferably of French loaf – and continue cooking until thoroughly done. Then add chopped parsley and onion tops.

Oysters may be added at this point if desired. Your dressing is now ready to insert.

Note: The above secret of drying and browning before seasoning may be applied to the cooking of all meats and will make them tender and juicy without water.

In the cooking of meats for stews, water of course is added after browning and cooking awhile with the seasoning.

MINCED BOLOGNA SANDWICHES

2 *cups bologna minced*
1/4 *cup chopped green pepper*
1/2 *teaspoon mustard*
1/4 *teaspoon salt*
1/8 *teaspoon pepper*
3 *tablespoons chopped pickle*
2 *tablespoons catsup*
1/2 *cup salad dressing*
   Bread

Combine ingredients in order given, mix thoroughly. Serve on lettuce between slices of bread spread with margarine.

HASH

Any leftover, or even freshly cooked meat may be used for hash.

3 *cups hot water*
2 *cups chopped meat*
4 *cups fresh potatoes, cut small*
1 *green or bell pepper*
2 *medium-sized onions*
1 *tablespoon tomato paste*

Put rounded tablespoon lard in hot iron skillet or pot, 1 heaping tablespoon flour, for "roux." Cook as usual, put in cut onions, browned slightly, add cut meat, cook 10 minutes, stirring, add 1 cup water, then other ingredients. Potatoes last: 1 hour cooking is sufficient. Any cold meat, chicken, turkey, cold pork roast, makes delicious hash if carefully made. Tomato paste can be left out if desired.

DAUBE GLACE

3 *pound beef round*
1 *medium-sized onion*
3 *pieces celery*
1/2 *clove garlic sliced thin*
1 *bay leaf*
3 *shallots*
1 *can Italian tomato paste*
1 *heaping tablespoon flour*
3 *tablespoons salad oil*
1/2 *envelope gelatin*

Remove from your daube all fat, gristle and strings.

Put on fire very large iron pot. This daube cannot be properly prepared in anything else.

Put in pot the oil and daube and fry slowly for 1 hour. Turn every few minutes to prevent burning and scratch bottom of pan. While this is cooking, prepare the seasoning.

Cut onions, shallots, celery and garlic. Open tomato paste. At the end of the hour, remove the daube from pot, put on plate until you are ready to put it back in the gravy you are now preparing to make. If the oil in the pot has been absorbed by the meat until there isn't enough to make a roux, add 2 more tablespoons of salad oil, add flour and stir until the roux is brown then add the sliced medium sized onion, 1/2 of the cut-up shallots and stir until the onions begin to brown. At this point add the tomato paste, and stir the mixture until all of the moisture is cooked out of the paste. Now is the time for a

cupful of boiling water, stirring continually until all is well mixed then add celery, the rest of the cut-up shallots, the bay leaf and garlic.

Be careful that all this does not burn. By this time, you must add a cup of hot water every few minutes and put the daube back in the gravy. Fill the pot to the top with boiling water, add 2 teaspoons salt and 1/2 teaspoon black pepper. Keep on low flame and cook until the meat can be cut easily with a spoon. Be careful to stir often. After cooking in the gravy for 2 hours, more than a quart of gravy should be left. Dissolve gelatin in half a cup of cold water, add to the gravy and place 2 medium sized whole boiled carrots lengthwise in the bottom of the dish in which you intend to mould the daube glace. A rectangular shaped pyrex bread pan is excellent. Pick the pieces of meat out of the gravy and lay them in the dish and pour everything that remains in the pot into the dish.

May be served hot or set on ice for several hours and serve on lettuce leaves on large platter. Slice edges with sharp knife and turn out on platter. This is an excellent Sunday night supper dish.

Serve with small hot biscuits. The method of making this dish is given in detail to enable the reader to prepare this delicious dish without fear of failure.

STEAK WITH MUSHROOM GRAVY

Remove from steak (tenderloin or sirloin, 2½ or 3 lbs.) gristle and string. Season on both sides with salt and pepper, place in hot deep fryer with just enough shortening to keep from sticking: fry quickly on both sides. Prepare one onion, sliced thin, 1 pod garlic, (1 bell pepper if available). Remove steak from frying pan and place on platter, then drop into same pan the above onions and seasoning stirring constantly while frying. When thoroughly brown, add 3 tablespoons tomato catsup, teaspoon Worcestershire sauce and 1 can mushrooms and a few sprigs parsley chopped fine. Cook this gravy for about 3 minutes adding a small quantity of water, then pour over the steak and serve hot.

CHICKEN A LA KING

4 cups diced chicken (cooked)
1 shredded green pepper
1 heaping tablespoon chopped
  mushrooms
2 tablespoons salad oil
3 tablespoons flour
¼ cup pimento, shredded
1 cup strained chicken soup

Put oil in skillet, heat and fry slow the peppers and mushrooms for 10 minutes. Remove them from the oil and add to oil first the flour, stirring to keep smooth, then the soup. Cook for 5 minutes, then add milk, mushrooms, pepper and pimento, salt and pepper. Put in double boiler if necessary to heat over again.

BAKED ROAST FOWL

Have fowl drawn and legs placed properly.

Chop liver, gizzard, heart into small pieces.

Fry in 4 even tablespoons salad oil until brown, then add 6 finely chopped shallots, 2 green peppers and 2 cups chopped celery, salt and pepper. Add 6 cups of stale bread, soaked and squeezed.

Chop, mash and mix well as you fry. Taste for seasoning, set aside till cool enough to handle. Stuff into fowl, and fill craw full.

Save 1 cup dressing for gravy.

Rub salt, pepper, salad oil on fowl, place in deep baking pan, bake for 1 hour until brown, then add water enough to half fill baking pan, add cup of dressing, mix well, and baste fowl with gravy every 15 minutes until thoroughly done.

CORNBREAD DRESSING (FOR DOMESTIC DUCK)

chopped giblet, heart and liver
¼ bunch shallots, or large onions
½ small pod garlic, sliced thin
3 cups cooked cornbread, crumbled
  salt, red and black pepper
1 sprig parsley
2 tablespoons salad oil

Put oil and chopped inners in iron skillet and fry brown. Add shallots, garlic, pepper. Fry brown for 10 minutes, add crumbled cornbread (cooked day before if possible), parsley. Mix and cook for 15 minutes, then cool sufficiently to stuff duck.

PLANTATION PORK SAUSAGE

10 pounds pork cut from loin (along backbone)
3 pounds fat cut from top of back
2 tablespoons sage
2 tablespoons black pepper
1 tablespoon ground red pepper

Cut pork loin and fat into small pieces and feed it to the sausage grinder alternately. This makes the final mixing much easier. When the meat is all ground, mix with seasoning, and set aside for a few hours. Fry a small piece – taste to determine if more sage and salt is necessary. Pack in crockery bowl and set on ice. Make into round flat cake, and fry when needed. Should keep 2 weeks.

PLANTATION HOGSHEAD CHEESE

1 whole hog's head, well cleaned
5 gallons water in large soup kettle
5 large onions
2 red peppers cut fine
parsley and shallots
1 pod garlic
1 tablespoon black pepper

Set kettle of water to boil, and put in at once your hog's head. Boil for 3 hours then take fork and see if it can be pulled apart easily. If not, boil one hour more. When it can be easily pulled apart, remove the head from liquid, place in large china or white granite-ware platter, pull all the bone out of the head, remove pieces of skin, and put the shredded meat into large bowl until you have finished with the whole head. All this must be done with the fingers, or one can

never be sure that all the small parts of bone have been removed.

Return the meat to kettle of liquid which should be reduced to about 1¹/₂ gallons by this time. Set on fire, and cut onions, shallots, parsley and garlic very fine, add to boiling kettleful. Boil 10 minutes, then add pepper, red peppers and salt. Boil for 1 hour more, but stir continually to prevent sticking and burning. Many a fine kettle has been scorched in the last hour of cooking. Taste for seasoning, add more if necessary, and pour into small china and glass bowls.

BAKED HAM WITH APPLESAUCE GLAZE

1 whole ham (8-10 lbs.)
Mustard
2 cups applesauce
1 cup brown sugar
Whole cloves for decorating
¹/₄ teaspoon ground cloves

Buy a fine quality, well-cured ham which does not require parboiling. Scrub it, rub surface with mustard and place fat side up in roasting pan. Bake in slow 300° F. oven until almost tender, allowing about 25 minutes per pound (little over 4 hours for 10-lb. ham). Forty-five minutes before ham is done, remove from oven, carefully cut off rind except a strip around the shank bone. Rub a little more mustard over fat, score it diagonally to form diamond-shaped pieces. Mix applesauce, brown sugar and ground cloves, spread over surface of ham. Insert whole cloves if desired. Return ham to oven, finish baking. During last 10 minutes, increase heat to 450° F. to form a nice crust.

BEEF OR VEAL GRILLADE

$1^{1}/_{2}$-2 *pounds beef or veal round*
      $^{1}/_{2}$ inch thick
   1 *large onion cut in rings*
   4 *tablespoons salad oil*
   3 *tablespoons flour*

This beef dish should be cooked in an hour and a half, and was used as a breakfast dish, served with grits.

Cut the round into pieces about 3 inches square: have oil in iron skillet very hot. Fry each piece until it is brown, remove from skillet into plate, and make roux with oil you have used in frying meat. Brown the roux, fry the onions, return meat to skillet, stir well with roux and onions, add two cups boiling water slowly, and serve soon as meat is tender.

Rapid cooking is necessary to give this dish the proper flavor, and it requires the all but undivided attention of a good Creole cook.

Serve with grits and hot biscuits.

VEAL LOAF

   2 *pounds veal*
$^{1}/_{2}$ *pound pork*
   2 *slices bread*
   1 *onion*
   3 *carrots*
   1 *pod garlic*
   1 *bell pepper*
   1 *stalk celery*

To the ground meat (run through meat chopper twice to have extra fine) add seasoning, salt, red pepper, black pepper, and work in bread that has been softened and squeezed dry, pack and work until it holds together, then dip, and roll in flour, and dust free of loose flour. Drop into lard enough to keep from sticking, and brown thoroughly all around, then drop around all the chopped onion, garlic, celery, bell pepper and carrots, and fry slowly. Cover with water and let cook (keeping covered) slowly about $1^{1}/_{2}$ hours until well done through loaf, turning occasionally, makes a delicious gravy, and the loaf does not break into pieces. Serve with rice or creamed potatoes.

Keeps several days in ice box and may be sliced cold.

CHICKEN LA LOUISIANE

   1 *chicken (boiled until tender)*

Disjoint the chicken, drain and fry golden brown. Then serve with the following sauce. (Retain the broth or consommé for the sauce.)

Sauce for the Above

   2 *tablespoons butter or shortening*
   1 *tablespoon flour*
   6 *stoned olives*
  12 *mushrooms*
   4 *artichoke hearts*
   1 *pint of the chicken consommé*
      salt and cayenne pepper to taste
      sherry

Melt the butter, remove from the fire and add the flour, stirring until smooth. Add about 1 pint of the consommé or broth of the chicken and cook to a creamy thickness. Then add the other ingredients and cook a few minutes longer.

CREOLE CROQUETTES

any leftovers (meats or poultry)
1 *tablespoon shortening*
1 *onion*
1 *pod garlic*
1 *stalk celery*
parsley to taste
1/2 *bell pepper*
1 *egg*
3 *boiled Irish potatoes*
1 *cup bread or cracker crumbs*
salt and cayenne pepper to taste

Run meat or poultry with vegetables through the meat chopper, then add the potatoes mashed. Season and stir in the beaten egg in the mixture. Shape in small balls, roll in cracker or bread crumbs, fry quickly in deep hot shortening until golden brown. Drain on heavy brown kraft paper. Serve hot.

EGG DUMPLING

2 *eggs beaten well*
1 *cup flour*
1 *teaspoon baking powder*
1 *pinch salt*
4 *tablespoons water*

Mix all together. Drop by spoonsful in gravy. Cover and cook until done.

QUAIL WITH WINE

1/2 *cup butter or margarine*
8 *quail*
2/3 *cup diced onion*
1 *teaspoon salt*
1/4 *teaspoon pepper*
2/3 *cup sherry*

Melt butter in skillet. Sauté quail until brown. Add onion; cook slowly until onion is wilted. Add salt, pepper and wine; bring to a boil. Simmer, cover 20 minutes. (These may be pressured 10 minutes, then finished in oven.)

Remember, water is never used in the cooking of wild game. Seems to bring out a wild taste. Dry roast or broil all birds and larger game with butter, and serve with sliced lemon and chopped parsley and use a little port or claret but never water.

DUMPLINGS FOR CHICKEN

Rich biscuit dough, cut in any shape desired, dropped into the gravy of chicken stew covered and steamed until done is very delicious when served hot.

BREADED VEAL ROUNDS

2 *pounds veal round, cut into*
   ¹/₂ steaks
2 *eggs*
3 *cups toasted and rolled bread*
   crumbs
2 *very thin slices garlic*
   Salt and black pepper

Cut all gristle and fat from your veal rounds, beat the eggs in plate, add garlic salt and pepper, dip meat in egg until well coated, then put one piece at a time in plate of bread crumbs, and fry in hot oil. Use iron skillet with 2 inches of oil. The meat should fry brown in about ten minutes. This makes a delicious meal served with mashed potatoes, a green vegetable and lettuce with Thousand Island dressing.

CHINESE CHOP SUEY

1 *quart pork or chicken cubed*
¹/₂ *cup chopped salt pork*
1 *pint water*
1 *onion chopped*
2 *cups celery cut 1 inch*
¹/₂ *tablespoon salt*
2 *tablespoons molasses sorghum*
3 *tablespoons flour*
3 *tablespoons water with flour*
¹/₂ *cup mushrooms*
2 *tablespoons Chinese sauce*

First fry salt pork, when brown put in meat and fry until brown, add water, onion, celery, salt. Let simmer one hour, then add mushrooms, molasses and Chinese sauce. Cook 10 minutes.

BOILED RICE

There are a great many people whose only idea of rice is a small mound of a gluey substance, which is served with different dishes in hotels and restaurants in the sections of the country where rice is so popular. If more people understood how to cook rice it would be appreciated as a delicious and nutritious food. With the gumbo and stews, recipes of which are to be given in this book, rice is a necessary part of the meal. In New Orleans and southern Louisiana, a housewife would not think of leaving rice off of her dinner menu. It is always served with meat dishes, and the delicious Creole dinner, red beans and rice, is very popular too as a luncheon dish.

For a family of six, take 1½ cups rice, and 3 pints water, and 1 teaspoon salt. Wash the rice in a little water, pour it off and put the rice in pot with the salt and water, and set on a low flame, so that it would take about fifteen minutes to come to a boil, then take up a grain and chew it. If there is a little hard spot left in the middle of the grain, the rice is not done. Continue to taste every minute or two, and as soon as the grain is done all the way through, take off the fire, pour off most of the water, then draw on and pour off the rice two pots cold water, pour rice into a colander, and set over a tall pot in which there are a few inches of slowly boiling water, and allow to steam for a half hour or less, if necessary. Never steam rice in a low pot. If the water, during the steaming process touches the rice, the rice will be soggy and not fit to eat. This method of cooking requires but a few minutes care, and never fails to give you a delicious dish of rice with every grain separate. The old Creole method of cooking rice, which I shall not give here, is a success only on a wood stove, in a thick iron pot. When cooked on the intense heat of a gas stove, it is more than apt to scorch.

STUFFED EGGPLANT (A LA CREOLE)

For a family of six, take the following:

3 large eggplants
3 medium-sized onions
3 green or bell peppers
3 cups soaked white bread squeezed dry
1 pound fresh or canned shrimp or fresh pork meat chopped fine
2 rounded tablespoons lard

Cut open lengthwise the eggplants. Boil in plenty of water for 2½ to 3 hours, take carefully out of water so they will break as little as possible, place cut side up on flat cake tins, and scoop out all the inside, leaving the shell to stuff. Have an iron skillet ready, put on stove. When hot, put in lard and chopped onion, let cook until edges of onions are brown, put in immediately shrimp or pork and eggplant, that you removed from shells – cook 10 minutes, add salt and pepper, then put in, stirring all the time, the bread and the chopped green pepper. Fry for 15 minutes more, then put in shells and sprinkle toasted bread crumbs over the tops, put in oven and bake for 20 minutes in hot oven. This is a delicious dish, and seldom used and cooked properly except in the Creole section of southern Louisiana. The shrimp or pork may be left out. This dish requires careful cooking.

SPAGHETTI A LA CREOLE

1 *pound small spaghetti*
1 *can Italian tomato paste*
6 *shallots or 1 large onion*
2-3 *large green peppers*
    salt, pepper and ½ pod garlic,
    sliced thin
2 *tablespoons salad oil*

To 2 quarts water add about a tablespoon of salt. Drop in spaghetti, boiling until done.

While this is boiling, prepare tomato sauce. Put in large iron skillet, oil and sliced onion. No roux with this recipe.

Fry until onion begins to brown, add salt, pepper, green peppers and tomato paste. Fry until a rather dry mass. At this point add 1 cup boiling water. Cook again until dry. Strain spaghetti through colander, add to tomato sauce, cook and stir for 10 minutes and serve. Oysters may be added to sauce to great advantage.

BUTTER BEANS A LA CREOLE

5 *cups hot water*
3 *pounds fresh green butter beans*
1 *level tablespoon lard or salad oil*

Shell the butter beans and wash. Make a roux in iron skillet, fry onion in roux until brown, add 5 cups hot water, change into stew pan, season with a little salt ½ teaspoon, boil slowly for 2 hours, add a little black pepper and a little more salt if necessary and serve. The water will have boiled down to a cupful by this time, and makes a delicious gravy to serve on rice.

CREOLE JAMBALAYA

This is the famous Creole – not French dish. Seems to be known only to the Creoles, and is with them a favorite dish for luncheon:

4 *cups boiled rice (page 36)*
½ *pound raw or boiled ham*
½ *pound small sausages, sliced*
2 *green peppers*
4 *green onions*
2 *medium dry onions*
    Salt and pepper
1 *can tomato paste*

The rice must be boiled before you start to make your jambalaya. Boil 1¾ cups rice, and have already cooling. Then put in iron skillet 2 tablespoons lard or bacon grease, fry chopped onion until edges begin to brown, add tomato paste or canned tomatoes, chopped green peppers, sausage and ham. Fry, stirring well all the time, for 15 or 20 minutes. Then add the boiled rice, turn gas down, cook slowly for almost an hour, stirring every now and then.

A simple lunch menu follows:

Head lettuce, with mayonnaise, Jambalaya, hot tea, lemonade or ice tea, toasted saltine crackers, and crab-apple, plum or mayhaw jelly.

FRIED PLANTAINS (CREOLE)

Three large plantains sliced lengthwise, ¼ inch thick. Fry in as little lard as possible, place on dish. Take clean iron skillet, put in 1 cup sugar, brown, put in 1 cup hot water, cook and stir until sugar caramel is melted; then put plantains in the syrup, and cook gently for fifteen minutes. Only the Creoles cook plantains this way.

STRING BEANS A LA CREOLE

The Creole cooks vegetables almost invariably with a slice of dry salt pork.

Take 2 pounds string beans prepare, put in pot with 3 pints cold water, slice of salt pork 1 inch thick, and cook slowly for 2 hours. Taste and add black pepper, and salt if needed. Cook for 30 minutes more, and serve.

The same method is used in cooking cabbage, which is invariably served with rice.

If using a waterless cooker drop snap beans into hot grease with all seasoning, cover and cook slowly without water. Should only take ½ hour to cook this way. If water becomes necessary only a half cup need be added. Snap beans retain their fresh flavor if cooked in a waterless cooker.

RED BEANS A LA CREOLE

Put one pound of red beans in two quarts of cold water (wash well first) and boil for one hour and a half on a slow fire. Then chop 2 medium sized onions or 8 or 10 young green onions, put 1 rounded tablespoon lard in skillet, and add heaping tablespoon flour for a "roux" – stir until dark brown, then stir in the onions, fry until the onions begin to brown at edges, add about a cup of the bean water, stir well until well mixed, then pour all this into the beans. Add salt and pepper enough to taste, let cook 20 minutes more, and serve with rice.

PUREE OF SPINACH

Put 2 large bunches of spinach in 1 pint hot water, boil for 30 minutes.

Put 1 tablespoon salad oil in iron skillet, make brown roux with heaping tablespoon flour, add spinach and water. Boil for 10 minutes more, season with salt and black pepper. Serve in deep dish with two hard-boiled eggs sliced thin on top.

SCALLOPED POTATOES

6 medium Irish potatoes
peel and slice them thin

Sprinkle with grated cheese, season with salt and pepper. Place into greased baking dish. Sprinkle again with more grated cheese. Cover with milk and a lump of butter and bake in hot oven until potatoes are tender.

CORN AU GRATIN

1 can corn
1 can tomatoes
2 large onions
1 cup chopped celery
2 sweet peppers
1 tablespoon lard
2 cups bread

Put lard in skillet with onions, fry till edges brown, add corn, tomatoes, peppers and celery, salt and pepper and fry fast for 10 minutes. Then add 2 cups soaked and squeezed bread, and fry for 10 minutes more, mixing and stirring well. Put in pudding pan, sprinkle with bread crumbs, bake for 20 minutes. This is delicious made with fresh corn cut from the cob. When it is ready to serve, sprinkle a handful of grated cheese over the top.

CARAMEL SWEET POTATOES

Take 4 large or 8 small sweet potatoes, put in pot of cold water to boil. When soft enough to stick a fork into, draw the water off, cool enough to handle, split in four sections lengthwise, and fry until brown in deep lard or frying oil. Drain on brown paper, a paper bag set on a dish is best, then put on hot fire or iron frying pan, or skillet. 1½ cups sugar, and stir until brown. Add two cups hot water, stirring until all lumps are dissolved, then boil down slowly for ten minutes, add the potatoes, cover, and simmer very slowly without stirring for fifteen minutes and serve.

PLANTATION POTATO PONE

I have named this dish Plantation Potato Pone because I have never seen it served anywhere except at the tables of sugar planters. It may be that it is known to many others, but not within my experience.

Grate about 6 large raw sweet potatoes, mix with 2 cups sugar, 1½ cups milk, and 2 teaspoons nutmeg. Bake in pudding pan for about 2½ hours. This pone requires rather a hot fire. It is a most delicious dish, but requires, in the grating, so much of the cook's time that it has not been used as much as it should be in these days of few servants. One may boil or bake the potatoes instead of grating them making it easier. In this case cream thoroughly, and add ½ lump of butter, and dash of cinnamon instead of nutmeg, and topped with marshmallows. You will need to bake only until the marshmallow topping is toasted.

SWEET POTATO CROQUETTES

Take 6 medium sized sweet potatoes, or enough for 4 teacups full after they are boiled and mashed, and set to boil until soft enough to stick a fork into, drain water off, set to cool until cool enough to handle. Peel, mash with potato masher, and set on ice for two hours, about the time you wish to use them. These croquettes must be fried as soon as made up, or they will get too soft to handle. Add to the cold mashed potatoes the following: 1 cup sugar, 1 teaspoon salt, 1 cup chopped pecans or walnuts. Make immediately with hands into the proper croquette shape, roll well in sifted flour, then fry immediately a nice brown in deep hot fat or frying oil.

These are delicious when served with stewed chicken and rice and gravy.

STUFFED POTATOES

Bake 4 large potatoes at 450° F. Cut in half lengthwise, scoop out insides and mash with pepper, salt, butter and a dash of parsley. When smooth add a little hot milk and melted butter and beat until white and fluffy. Refill the potato shells. Sprinkle with paprika or grated cheese and return to hot oven until brown.

≈≈ ≈≈ ≈≈ ≈≈ ≈≈ ≈≈ ≈≈

A handful of chopped shallots and spoonful of chopped parsley should be added to meat or fish gravy half an hour before serving the dish.

FRENCH FRIED POTATOES

Cut pared potatoes into lengthwise strips about $1/2$ inch wide. Soak them in cold water. Drain thoroughly. Dry as much as possible, place them in a wire basket and plunge it into deep shortening, heated until a cube of bread browns in 20 seconds (390-400° F.). Fry until well browned and thoroughly cooked in center (test by removing 1 strip with a fork). Drain on paper, salt and serve hot. Do not try to fry too many potatoes at a time. It is quicker in the end to fry several small batches than one large batch which overcrowds the kettle. The potatoes fried first may be kept war in the oven while the others are being fried. Be sure to have enough fat to more than cover the potatoes during frying.

RICE AND EGG (BREAKFAST DISH)

2-3 *cups cooked rice (page 36)*
  2 *eggs*

Beat eggs, pour in rice, stir well. Add $1/2$ teaspoon salt and pepper (black preferred). Put 1 level tablespoon lard in frying pan, heat well, and fry rice and egg until it is dry – about 5 minutes. This is a delicious dish.

PLANTATION SQUASH CAKES

3 *cups boiled squash mashed when*
   cold
1 *egg*
1 *teaspoon baking powder*
1 *cup sugar*
  Pinch salt

Mix the above and add enough flour to make batter a little thicker than required for batter cakes. Fry like batter cakes, sprinkle with sugar and serve with meat dish for luncheon or dinner.

You may use eggplants instead of squash.

STUFFED PEPPERS

12 *large green sweet peppers*
 2 *large onions*
 1 *tablespoon lard*
 2 *cups soaked bread, squeezed dry*
    or cooked rice
 1 *small slice garlic*

If $1/4$ pound of ground pork meat is added to stuffing it adds to the flavor.

Chop onions and 6 peppers, small, fry for 10 minutes in lard, add salt and pepper, then add bread, fry 10 minutes more. Cut in halves the 6 peppers and stuff with this mixture; put toasted bread crumbs on top and bake for 15 minutes in hot oven and serve.

The medium sized red skin onion is superior in taste to the larger white skin varieties. The red onion is used in Creole cookery.

Ground meat or shrimp that has been fried with seasoning adds a wonderful flavor to stuffed peppers, eggplants, squash or tomatoes.

STEWED CORN A LA CREOLE

Eight well-developed ears corn, split grains with sharp knife, cut off top of grains first, then cut the rest off, and scrape cob. Make roux Creole fashion with 1 level tablespoon lard, 1 level tablespoon flour. Fry brown, add 2 chopped onions, fry as directed, add corn, stir and fry 15 minutes, then add from time to time 3 cups water. Cook slowly, stirring often, season well.

SOUFFLES POTATOES AU GRATIN

Take large firm potatoes, peel and wipe them dry, slice them evenly about $1/8$-inch thick, dry each slice in a towel. Have 2 large pots of kidney beef lard, the deeper pot very hot but not boiling. Drop 1 slice in this, if the lard does not bubble it is not hot enough. When it is hotter put in potatoes, moving them for about 4 minutes. Then drop cupful at a time into boiling fat in the second pot. Leave them until they are puffed (souffles) which occurs very soon. Remove from fire, keep in warm place while others cook, then add salt.

"A SECRET"

To Make Celery Crisp As A Cracker

Wash and cut an Irish potato in about six pieces drop into a container with the celery – cover with water and place in refrigerator. It will crispen even old celery like magic.

FRENCH FRIED ONIONS

$1/2$ cup milk
$1/2$ cup flour
1 teaspoon melted shortening
$1/2$ teaspoon salt
1 egg yolk

Make thin batter as for fritters.

Cut large onions across into slices about one-fourth inch thick. Separate the slices into rings. Dip the rings into a thin batter. Place in a frying basket and fry in shortening at 360 to 370° F. until delicately browned. Drain. Salt lightly before serving. If preferred, onion slices may be simply dipped in milk and dredged with flour instead of coated with batter.

NUT AND POTATO CROQUETTES

2 cups hot mashed potatoes
$1/4$ cup cream or milk
$1/2$ teaspoon salt
$1/8$ teaspoon pepper
few grains cayenne
yolk of 1 egg
$1/3$ cup chopped pecan nut meats
$1/2$ teaspoon Royal baking powder

Mix all ingredients with fork until light. Shape as for croquettes. Roll in bread crumbs. Dip in egg which has been mixed with a little cold water. Roll in bread crumbs again and fry in deep hot fat at 385° F. until brown. Drain on unglazed paper and serve.

Nuts may be left out.

SPINACH CASSEROLE

3 boxes chopped spinach
1 8-ounce Philadelphia cream
* cheese*
1 can water chestnuts chopped
2 cans hearts of artichokes (large)
1½ sticks butter or oleo
* Italian bread crumbs*

Soften cream cheese and butter. Cook spinach about 1 minute. Drain well. Chop chestnuts fine. Drain artichoke hearts and cut in half or ⅓ and line bottom of 10 inch Corning skillet. Mix spinach, cream cheese, butter and chestnuts, place on top of artichoke hearts, sprinkle with bread crumbs. Bake at 350° until bubbly.

CREAMED CAULIFLOWER

Wash cauliflower and remove sections from stem. Put to boil with salt to taste. Cook until tender, drain and serve in White Sauce pan (page 20).

FRIED SWEET POTATOES

Large Louisiana yams – peel – cut into slices about ½ inch thick, and 1 inch wide. Soak in cold salted water an hour or more. Drain, dry and place in lightly greased pan in slow oven (not crowded) turning at intervals until browned and tender (sugar and butter may be added to taste). Can be served with pork or beef roast.

≈≈ ≈≈ ≈≈ ≈≈ ≈≈ ≈≈ ≈≈ ≈≈ ≈≈

Cabbage when slightly parboiled and drained, then cooked in waterless cooker without any shortening or fats is delicious and very easily digested. It may be served as a salad with French dressing or as a vegetable dish with tomato sauce.

MAYONNAISE

(This will keep a week and will never curdle.)

- ³/₄ cup vinegar
- 1 cup water
- Yolks of 2 eggs
- 5 heaping teaspoons flour
- 1 pint salad oil
- 2 teaspoons celery salt
- 2 teaspoons salt

Mix flour carefully to prevent lumping with ¹/₂ cup water. Put the other half cup water in small pot, and when it boils, pour in, stirring well the flour and water mixture. Let boil about 3 minutes, take from fire, and pour over the beaten yolks, and slowly beat into this half the oil, then add salt and celery salt and ¹/₂ cup vinegar. Beat well, then slowly add, beating all the time, the rest of the oil and vinegar. Put in glass and cover with glass top, not metal, and put in cool place. This mayonnaise won't separate or curdle and will keep for a week.

STUFFED TOMATO SALAD

Six large smooth tomatoes, dipped for half minute in fast boiling water. Remove skins, set on ice twenty minutes. Use half cup each chopped celery, green peppers and shredded lettuce. Mix in half teaspoon salt and 2 tablespoons mayonnaise. Scoop out middles of tomatoes, add this to mixture, chopped fine, fill tomatoes, crown with 1 teaspoon mayonnaise, place on lettuce leaf and serve.

CREOLE POTATO SALAD

- 6 ice-cold boiled potatoes
- 2 cups mayonnaise
- 2 young green onions
- 2 hard-boiled eggs
- 1 large stalk celery
- 2 green peppers
- 4 green pickles
- ¹/₂ teaspoon black pepper

Slice potatoes, cut celery fine, chop all other ingredients, mix in china or earthenware bowl, add pepper, mayonnaise, salt, juice ¹/₂ lemon or lime, and mix. Put on ice for two hours, then serve generous portions on large lettuce leaf.

TARTAR SAUCE

- 1 cup mayonnaise
- 2 sour cucumber pickles
- 1 green onion chopped fine

Chop cucumbers fine and mix well together.

THOUSAND ISLAND DRESSING

- ¹/₂ cup mayonnaise
- ¹/₂ cup tomato catsup

Mix and serve cold on head lettuce.

FRENCH DRESSING

- 2 tablespoons salad oil
- 1 tablespoon vinegar
- ¹/₂ teaspoon sugar
- pinch mustard
- salt and black pepper

ITALIAN TOMATO SAUCE

1 large onion or bunch shallots, chopped fine
1 can Italian tomato paste
1 pod garlic, sliced thin
2 cups chicken broth
Salt and pepper
2 tablespoons salad oil

Fry onions and garlic in oil until nearly brown, add tomato paste, fry 10 minutes, add chicken broth and season well.

Serve a plateful of plain boiled spaghetti. Sprinkle with Italian cheese, then pour sauce over all. Be sure to have everything hot. This is the famous Italian dish. Serve claret with this and consider this a meal.

AVOYELLES COCKTAIL SAUCE

(Mrs. Geo. L. Mayer, Jr.)

1/2 lemon (juice)
1 cup tomato sauce
2 tablespoons Worcestershire sauce
1 tablespoon pepper sauce
1/2 cup celery finely chopped
2 tablespoons horseradish

Mix thoroughly and place over shrimp in cocktail glasses. Serve with crisp crackers and lettuce salad if desired.

Celery may be left out when served with oysters or soup meat.

SHRIMP COCKTAIL

Use 8 shrimp to a glass and serve with avoyelles cocktail sauce (above).

JELLIED PICKLE RELISH SALAD

1 package lime gelatin
1 3/4 cups boiling water
Canned white asparagus tips
1 cup pickle relish
2 cups salmon salad
Watercress
French dressing

Dissolve gelatin in boiling water, cool. When it begins to set, coat desired mold with thin layer of gelatin. Fill mold with alternate layers of asparagus, relish and salmon salad. Pour rest of gelatin over it. Chill. Turn onto bed of watercress marinated with French dressing.

MOLDED BARTLETT SALAD

2 packages lemon gelatin
2 cups boiling water
Large pear halves
Salad dressing
Large black cherries
1 3/4 cups pear juice and water
Avocado balls
Watercress
Whipped cream

Dissolve gelatin in boiling water, add fruit juice and chill. In large ring mold, space black cherries so that a pear cavity will fit over each. Pour in gelatin and allow to set. Unmold onto chop plate. Garnish outside of ring with watercress and arrange avocado balls over it. Fill center of ring with mixed half-and-half salad dressing and whipped cream.

VEGETABLE SALAD

1 cup finely cut cabbage
1 cup cold boiled beets
1 cup cold boiled carrots
1 cup finely cut celery
1 cup cold boiled potatoes
¹/₂ cup pimientos
1 head lettuce
1 cup French dressing

Soak cabbage in cold water 1 hour; drain and add beets, carrots, potatoes and celery. Mix well together, season with salt and pepper and serve on lettuce leaves. On top put strips of pimiento and serve with French dressing, to which may be added one teaspoon onion juice.

LAKE SHRIMP SALAD

6 pounds boiled lake shrimp
1 cup mayonnaise
5 cups cut-up celery

Boil shrimp in gallon of water, and season with bay leaf, 1 slice onion, and 3 small slices from pod of garlic and heaping teaspoon salt. Taste shrimp to ascertain if well cooked. When done, turn gas off, and let stand in water for 10 minutes, then turn into colander.

When cool enough to handle, peel and put in bowl, mix with cut celery, mayonnaise and 3 pieces of shallot tops. Serve on lettuce leaf and top with more mayonnaise.

COLE SLAW

1 nice green cabbage
1 cup mayonnaise

Mix well after shredding cabbage fine, put on ice for an hour and serve.

CRAB SALAD

4 cups picked crab meat
2 cups cut-up celery
1 cup mayonnaise

Mix crab meat with celery and 1 cup mayonnaise. Add whatever salt and black pepper necessary, and serve on lettuce leaf, with additional mayonnaise.

CHICKEN SALAD

1 cold boiled hen or rooster
6 cups cut-up celery
2 cups mayonnaise

Cut the chicken pieces size you desire, season with salt and pepper, add 2 cups mayonnaise, and the cut-up celery, mix and serve on lettuce, topped with a teaspoon of mayonnaise. Decorate with sliced hard-boiled eggs.

APPETIZER

1 can sardines
6 olives
1 lemon
1 teaspoon tabasco pepper sauce

Remove bone and tail from sardine, put into a bowl with the chopped olives, tabasco sauce and the juice of one lemon. Spread on a fresh salty cracker, serve at luncheons with iced or hot tea, or as an appetizer before a meal.

CRAB COCKTAIL

Use to each cocktail ¹/₂ glass crab-meat, shredded lettuce and cocktail sauce with thin slice lemon. Put crab-meat in top of glass.

TUNAFISH SALAD

1 can tuna fish
2 hard-boiled eggs
4 stalks celery
1/2 cup mayonnaise
     Dash olive oil & vinegar

Put tuna fish into a deep dish. Add the chopped celery and hard-boiled eggs. Season to taste, a dash of olive oil and vinegar and mayonnaise. Serve on lettuce leaves, as chicken salad, it is practically just as nice and much cheaper to make.

FRUIT SALAD

1 cantaloupe cut in cubes $^1/_2$ inch in size
3 oranges cut up same size
3 bananas cut up same size
1 can pineapple, cut up
1 can white cherries
2 tablespoons white wine if desired
$^1/_2$ cup sugar

Mix sugar, wine and pineapple juice in bowl and cut bananas first, then other fruit. Put in refrigerator until thoroughly chilled. Serve in fruit cups if desired or on lettuce leaves topped with teaspoonful stiff mayonnaise.

COCKTAIL SAUCE

4 parts tomato catsup
1 part chili sauce
4 drops hot pepper sauce

Shredded lettuce for bottom cocktail glass, and slice lemon, 1 teaspoon horseradish.

OYSTER COCKTAIL

4 oysters in cocktail glass

Count your guests, then buy your oysters.
Put in cocktail glasses, tablespoon shredded lettuce, 3 tablespoons cocktail mixture given on page 44 omitting the horseradish if desired and 4 medium-sized oysters and serve very cold.
May also be served with following sauce.

REMOULADE SAUCE

$^1/_2$ cup mayonnaise
$^1/_2$ cup Creole mustard
$^3/_4$ cup olive oil
$^1/_2$ cup finely chopped celery
$^1/_2$ cup finely chopped onion
2 tablespoons minced parsley
2 tablespoons finely chopped dill pickle
2 cloves garlic minced
2 tablespoons horseradish
1 tablespoon paprika
   Juice of one lemon
   Few drops hot pepper sauce
   Red pepper to taste
2 tablespoons catsup

Blend first 3 ingredients. Then add others and blend in blender.

ROLLS AND BREAD

1 yeast cake
½ cup sugar
2 cups lukewarm milk (boiled)
2 teaspoons cinnamon
1 teaspoon salt
5 cups flour, measured before sifting
   Lard, size of a small egg

Put yeast cake, sugar, milk and spice to soak together for 10 minutes while you sift your flour into a bowl and work the lard into the flour until it is all crumbled well. Then add salt and the milk and yeast mixture. Work well together, and cover with a dusting of sifted flour, then cover bowl and set in a corner free from drafts to rise. The necessary time for rising is governed by the temperature. In summer rolls rise in an hour, in winter they take much longer. When the dough appears to have doubled its size take a spoon and work it down again to the original size, then put to rise again, and proceed as before. The second time they rise and are worked down is the time to make them into rolls or bread as desired. As you roll each roll into desired size, roll for a minute in melted lard, and place in baking pan. When your bread or roll pan is full leave room for rolls or bread to double its size. Sprinkle sugar and cinnamon on top, leave to rise, watch carefully. When they have doubled in height put in fairly hot oven and bake about 40 minutes. You must use your judgment. Bread making is an art, but very easy to do. Again experiment.

From this simple foundation recipe many delicious rolls and breads can be made. Add a package of raisins for raisin bread, or two cups full of chopped nuts for nut bread.

CONFEDERATE PUDDING

1 quart or pot of boiling grits
1 egg, beaten well
1 cup milk

Beat ingredients together, bake in hot oven for 40 minutes. Supper.

WAFFLES

2 cups flour
1½ cups milk
2 eggs (beaten separately)
2 tablespoons sugar
3 teaspoons baking powder
½ teaspoon salt
6 tablespoons melted butter

Sift flour, sugar, salt and baking powder into mixing bowl. Beat yolks well and add milk and beat, adding this to the flour slowly beating until perfectly smooth. Then add melted butter and fold in whites stiffly beaten. If desired, thinly sliced pieces of apple may be added.

Put strips of bacon over waffle plate and drop waffle dough over them and bake for bacon waffles.

NUT BREAD

4 cups flour
1 cup sugar
1½ cup chopped nuts
1 cup sweet milk
1 egg (beat white separately)
4 level teaspoons baking powder

Put into greased loaf bread pan and let stand for 40 minutes to rise. Bake in moderate oven.

BANANA QUICK BREAD

½ cup shortening
½ teaspoons salt
1 cup sugar
2 eggs, beaten
2 cups sifted flour
1 teaspoon soda
3 bananas, crushed
1 cup pecan meats

Cream shortening, salt and sugar. Add eggs, sifted flour and soda, banana pulp and nut meats. Bake in well-greased loaf pan in moderate 350° F. oven 40 minutes.

POP-OVERS

2 cups sifted flour
2 cups milk
2 eggs
1 teaspoon salt
2 heaping teaspoons baking powder

Mix well, fill muffin pans half full and bake in hot oven for 15 to 20 minutes.

VIRGINIA CORNBREAD

1 cup corn meal
1 cup sifted flour
2 tablespoons lard or butter
1 cup milk
2 level tablespoons sugar
2 eggs beaten separately
3 level teaspoons baking powder
Pinch salt

Beat sugar with eggs yolks, add corn meal, milk and flour, then melted lard or butter, then egg whites and baking powder and salt. Bake in greased tin pan in hot oven and cut into large squares.

OLE MISS CORNBREAD

3 cups cornmeal
3 cups sifted flour
3 cups milk
3 round tablespoons lard
6 even tablespoons sugar
4 eggs beaten separately
4 even teaspoons baking powder
1 teaspoon salt

Sift flour and cornmeal into bowl, in another bowl cream lard, sugar and salt together add yolks of eggs. Put milk into bowl with flour and meal, beat well, then pour into bowl of beaten eggs, add well beaten whites of eggs, and baking powder, pour into deep pan and bake in hot oven.

NEW ORLEANS CORNBREAD

3 cups corn meal
2 tablespoons lard or oil
2 cups boiling water
　Heaping teaspoon baking powder
¾ cup milk
　Teaspoon salt
1 egg

Put corn meal, lard, salt in bowl, set water to boil and as soon as it boils, pour on meal, stir and mix well, add milk, and put to cool for 40 minutes. After it is cool, add egg and baking powder, put in shallow tin pan or muffin rings, and bake in hot oven for about 30 minutes. This makes a crusty cornbread – very good.

BREAKFAST PUFFERS

2 *tablespoons butter*
2 *tablespoons sugar*
1 *cup milk*
2 *eggs, beaten separately*
2¼ *cups flour*
3½ *level teaspoons baking powder*

Beat sugar, butter, eggs together, add flour, milk, egg whites, baking powder, beat well, turn into buttered muffin pans, and bake 15 or 20 minutes in hot oven.
Double recipe for more than 3 people.

BANANA, APPLE OR ORANGE FRITTERS

1 *cup flour*
1¼ *teaspoons baking powder*
¼ *teaspoon salt*
1 *egg, beaten*
⅓ *cup milk*
2 *teaspoons shortening, melted*
   Orange sections seeded or sliced
   bananas or apples
1 *tablespoon lemon juice*
2 *tablespoons sugar*

Sift flour, baking powder and salt. Combine egg, milk and shortening, add to dry ingredients. Drop chopped fruit into the batter and fry in deep shortening (375° F.) about 5 minutes, or until brown. Sprinkle with sugar while still steaming.

OLD FASHIONED RUSK

Use recipe for bread given on page 47 and after it has risen once, work down and add the following:

4 *eggs, well beaten*
1 *teaspoon mace*
½ *teaspoon lemon extract*
2 *teaspoons cinnamon*

Beat well into dough, and add 1 cup sifted flour in addition to spice, etc.
Set to rise again. When doubled in bulk work down again, and set to rise for last time. Work down when doubled in bulk, place on lightly floured board, cut off pieces of uniform size with sharp knife, and put in well-buttered baking pan, brush with melted butter, mix with 1 tablespoon sugar. Set to rise. When double in size, put in moderate oven, and bake about 40 minutes.

SALLY LUNN

1 *cup sugar*
1 *pint sweet milk*
4 *cups sifted flour*
3 *eggs*
1 *heaping tablespoon melted butter*
3 *teaspoons baking powder*
   Pinch salt

Have milk lukewarm, mix with butter. Beat yolks, sugar well, add milk and butter mixture, then flour and beaten egg whites, baking powder. Bake in moderate oven, in shallow tin about one-half hour, serve hot and cut into squares at table.

HOT BISCUITS

5 cups flour, measured before sifting
1 cup lard
1½ cups milk
3 heaping teaspoons baking powder
1 teaspoon salt

Mix lard in sifted flour with fingers well, add salt, baking powder and milk. Flours differ in the milk they will take up – so this amount of milk may, with some flours be too much, or with other flours, too little, so use your own judgment. Mix well, roll half inch thick, cut with round cutter, bake in greased tins in fairly hot oven and serve hot. You may use 3 tablespoons condensed milk and 1⅓ cup water mixed.

Many housewives complain they can't make good biscuits no matter what recipe is used. This is due to the fact that too much flour is used to make up the biscuits on the board, and that biscuits are always better if allowed to rise after they are cut out for a half hour before baking. It is not everyone who has the "happy hand" with hot breads, but those who have not may easily learn with experiment-ing. Never use hot milk or water in making up biscuits. The baking powder gets into action too soon, and the result is a flat, prematurely risen biscuit.

NEW ORLEANS CORN PONE

3 cups corn meal
1½ cups boiling water
2 level tablespoons lard
1 teaspoon salt
1 cup milk
1 egg
2 teaspoons baking powder

Put meal, lard and salt in bowl, pour in boiling water, and stir until well mixed. Add milk and egg, set aside to cool for an hour, then beat well, add baking powder, and pour into greased pans, or muffin rings. Don't try to have more than two inches thick. Bake in hot oven for 40 minutes.

"FEATHERBEDS"

3 tablespoons shortening
1 tablespoon butter
1 cup lukewarm milk
1 yeast cake, broken
1½ tablespoons sugar
½ teaspoon salt
1 egg, well beaten
3 cups flour

Mix ingredients in order given and allow to rise. Cut down and let come up again, then break off small pieces, roll and put into greased muffin pans. Let rise. Bake in hot 425° F. oven about 20 minutes.

In the days when the French Quarter of New Orleans was built, the civilized world believed firmly that fevers, typhoid, malaria and the dreaded yellow fever rose from the ground, so most of the living and sleeping quarters were on the upper floor, and the ground floor was given over to shops, and the back part of the lower floor contained the stables and sleeping quarters for the many negro servants.

Front gates such as this, marked the entrance to the driveway. A winding stairway in the middle of the house came down to the driveway, for no Creole lady would have entered or left her carriage from the street. The kitchen was upstairs, separated from dining room and living quarters by a gallery. The odors of food, long in cooking after the French fashion, and the chattering of the many servants, were thus removed far enough from the dining and living room to preclude any possibility of annoyance to the dweller within.

The kitchen was always very large, and on the back of an enormous woodstove, the gumbo simmered and the rice and daube a la Creole cooked slowly, and the turbaned negroes moved slowly back and forth adding a little salt, or a handful of fine chopped onions and peppers to an already delicious dish.

In the dining room there was often a wooden fan-like arrangement, pulled slowly back and forth by a small black boy, to keep the breeze moving, and too most important, to keep the flies off the table, for there were no screened windows in that time.

NOTE – All cakes made with butter or shortening always cream butter and sugar first then if yolks of eggs are called for add yolks. Milk, flour and extract is added alternately. If whites only are called for (not yolks) cream butter and sugar as above, add milk and flour alternately and then *fold* in the beaten whites and *bake*.

≋≋≋≋≋≋≋≋≋≋≋≋≋≋≋≋≋≋≋≋≋≋

EGGS ON TOAST
(Will You Fool 'Em)

Quick and lovely in taste and looks is this dessert –

1 *pound cake*
1 *large can peach halves*
$^1/_2$ *pint whipping cream*

Place peach halves on sliced cake (toasted if desired) with rounded part up, encircle peach with whipped cream slightly sweetened.

WHITE CAKE
(LAYER OR LOAF)

1 *cup egg whites*
$2^1/_2$ *cups sugar*
1 *cup butter*
1 *cup milk*
5 *cups sifted flour*
$2^1/_2$ *teaspoons baking powder*
1 *teaspoon vanilla or almond essence*

Proceed as with any other cake, cream butter and sugar together and stiffly beaten egg whites alternately with flour, then baking powder, milk, vanilla or other extract. This cake is nice either as a layer or loaf, and is very good with filling for Favorite Lemon Pie.

Yolks left over may be used in sponge or devil's food cake or custard ice cream.

OLD-FASHIONED
SPONGE CAKE

24 *eggs*
$2^1/_2$ *pounds sugar*
$1^3/_4$ *pounds flour*
1 *cup water*
2 *heaping teaspoons baking powder*
2 *teaspoons vanilla essence*
1 *teaspoon salt*

This cake has come down from colonial days, is very delicious, and will serve 30 people. Baked in shallow square pans, cut in squares when cold and ice. Beat yellows of eggs well, slowly add, beating all the time, the sugar, until the mixture is creamy. Sift flour and add slowly first a cup full of flour, then some of the whites, which have been beaten stiff, then the cup of cold water and baking powder. Bake in moderate oven, allow to stand for several hours, then remove from pan, cut in squares, if desired, and ice.

SPONGE CAKE

6 *eggs*
2 *cups sugar*
$3^1/_2$ *cups sifted flour*
4 *tablespoons cold water*
  Vanilla essence
1 *teaspoon baking powder*
  Quick oven

LADY FINGERS

4 ounces flour
5 eggs
4 ounces powdered sugar

Put sugar and yolks in bowl and beat until very light. Add flour, then well beaten whites. Bake on white paper well greased, placed in tin pan. Drop batter in desired shape inch apart. Moderate oven.

MARBLE CAKE

Use recipe Simple Pudding Cake, put ½ of cake dough in large shallow tim square pan, add half cup cocoa to rest of dough, and stir in irregular designs through the dough in pan. Bake in moderate oven.

SPONGE LAYER

1 cup sugar
3 eggs
½ cup cold water
2 cups sifted flour
1 heaping teaspoon baking powder

Proceed to make as directions given for other sponge cake, bake in two layers, in moderate oven. Cut each layer in half, and put one cup rich custard between and sprinkle each top with powdered sugar. This makes two cakes.

SUNSHINE CAKE

6 eggs
1¼ cup sugar
1 cup flour
⅓ teaspoon cream of tartar
Pinch salt

Beat egg yolk till lemon color. Then add salt to egg whites and beat a little. Add cream of tartar and beat until very stiff. Sift sugar and add to beaten yolks, then egg whites, ½ teaspoon vanilla, and fold in flour lightly. Pour in wet tube pan and bake in moderate oven for about 30 minutes. Invert pan and remove cake when cold.

STRAWBERRY SHORTCAKE

3 eggs
2 cups flour
1 cup sugar
1 tablespoon butter
2 level teaspoons baking powder
Pinch salt

Prepare dough as instructed on page 52.

Flavor with vanilla, bake in tin layer cake pans, cut open when done with sharp knife, put between layers, 3 pints strawberries, mixed with 1 cup sugar.

COOKED ICING

1¹/₂ cups sugar
 5 even tablespoons cold water
 2 unbeaten egg whites
 2 teaspoons light-colored corn syrup
 1 teaspoon vanilla or almond
    extract

Put above in top of double boiler. Beat. Have boiling water in bottom of double boiler.

Use rotary egg beater entirely.

After beating constantly for 7 or 8 minutes over rapidly boiling water, the icing will be stiff enough to stand alone. Take from fire, flavor, and spread on cake. If it gets too stiff, add a teaspoon cold water.

CHOCOLATE PUFF CAKES

These make a delicious dessert and can be prepared in a hurry for unexpected guests.

 1 cup water
 5 eggs
¹/₂ cup butter
 1 pint sifted flour

Put water and butter in aluminum pot, bring to a boil, then stir in slowly 1 pint sifted flour. Keep on low flame and stir until mixture leaves the side of the pot. Remove from fire, stir until cool, then beat into the mixture 5 eggs, one at a time, beating all the time. Put in baking pans in shape of eclairs, bake in rather hot oven and when baked and cool, ice with cooked chocolate icing.

WHITE MOUNTAIN CAKE

 1 pound sugar
 1 pound flour
 1 pound butter
10 egg whites
 2 heaping teaspoons baking powder
   Pinch salt
 1 teaspoon almond extract.

Prepare dough as instructed on page 52.

Bake in layer pans, and put icing and grated cocoanut between layers.

SIMPLE PUDDING CAKE

 5 eggs
 1 cup butter or substitute
2¹/₂ cups sugar
 1 cup milk
6¹/₄ cups flour
 1 teaspoon vanilla
 3 heaping teaspoons baking powder

Proceed as with any other cake. Slice hot, if desired, and serve with sauce below.

 1 quart milk
³/₄ cup flour
 1 cup sugar
 1 cup whiskey

Put milk in double boiler when hot. Add flour dissolved in a little water, add sugar. Stir and cook until thickened, add whiskey and serve with cake.

SILVER CAKE

$^1/_2$ cup butter
$1^1/_2$ cups sugar
   Whites 8 eggs
1 cup milk
3 cups sifted flour
2 teaspoons baking powder

Prepare dough as instructed on page 52.

If you make custard ice cream, use egg whites for this cake.

DEVILS FOOD

1 cup butter
2 cups sugar
4 cups flour
1 cup milk
3 eggs
2 teaspoons baking powder

Proceed as with any other cake, then sprinkle 6 heaping tablespoons of cocoa or cut chocolate. Bake in moderate oven and ice with white icing (page 63).

IMPERIAL CAKE

1 pound butter
1 pound flour
1 pound sugar
$^1/_2$ pound chopped citron
9 eggs
2 teaspoons baking powder
1 pound blanched almonds chopped

Prepare dough as instructed on page 52.

Flavor with juice and grated rind of one lemon. Bake in round cake pan with tube in slow oven.

CREOLE BEAUTY CAKE

$^2/_3$ cup shortening
$^3/_4$ teaspoon salt
1 teaspoon almond extract
$1^1/_2$ cup sugar
   Pink coloring
$^3/_4$ cup chopped blanched almonds
3 cups sifted cake flour
$3^1/_2$ teaspoons baking powder
1 cup milk
4 egg whites, beaten fluffy, not stiff
$^1/_2$ cup cut maraschino cherries

Combine shortening, salt and flavoring, add sugar gradually and cream well. Sift flour and baking powder 3 times, add to creamed mixture alternately with liquid. Fold beaten egg whites into mixture. To $^2/_3$ of batter add pink coloring and almonds, pour into 2 greased 8-inch layer pans. To remaining batter add cherries, pour into third 8-inch layer pan. Bake in moderate 350° F. oven 30 minutes.

Then cover with white or colored icing.

COOKED ICING

2 cups granulated sugar
1 cup water
2 whites of eggs, beaten stiff

Boil sugar and water on low fire until a drop of the mixture will harden when dropped into a cup of cold water. Remove from fire, pour immediately, slowly into the beaten whites, beating all the time. Beat until thick enough to ice your cake. If the mixture hardens too fast, put a tablespoon of cold water in it, and it will spread evenly again, as when hot. Flavor as desired, $^1/_2$ teaspoon extract.

ANGEL FOOD

1½ cups sugar, sifted several times
1 cup sifted flour
1 tablespoon cold water into egg
   whites before beating
   Whites of 11 eggs
¼ teaspoon salt
1 teaspoon vanilla
½ teaspoon of almond extract
1 teaspoon cream of tartar

Beat egg whites to a stiffness that you can cut with a knife, add flour slowly, folding all the time, then extracts, cream of tartar, and bake in moderate oven in round cake pan with tube. Turn cake pan upside down on plate, and the cake will fall out of pan when cold.

RICE PUDDING

2 cups cooked rice
1 pint milk
1½ cups sugar
3 eggs
1 teaspoon vanilla
1 tablespoon cornstarch

Beat yolks of eggs well, add sugar slowly, beat until mixture is creamy, add milk slowly, pinch of salt, and put mixture in double boiler. Then add the cooked rice. When mixture is hot add cornstarch dissolved in a little water, and stir until thick. Take off fire, add vanilla, put in pudding pan, beat the whites of the eggs until stiff, add slowly one cup of sugar, a few drops of vanilla, spread on pudding, and bake in slow oven for about 15 minutes when meringue should be brown. Most people think this pudding is better cold, but some like it hot.

CREAM PUFFS

1 cup flour, measure before sifting
½ cup butter or oleo
1 cup water
5 eggs

Set water and butter on stove, and as soon as it boils, stir the flour in, and continue to stir until the paste leaves the side of the pot. Take off stove, allow to cool, then beat in one at a time, the 5 eggs (do not separate the eggs) and add a small pinch of soda. Drop into greased pans with a teaspoon and bake in moderate oven until they are a light brown. Don't take them out of the pans until they are cold. When cold, fill with the following custard made in double boiler:

2 cups of milk
   Yolks of 2 eggs
1 cup sugar
2 level tablespoons cornstarch
   dissolved in ½ cup water
2 teaspoons vanilla

If you want chocolate eclairs, add heaping tablespoon ground chocolate to the custard filling when hot, and mould the dough in long eclair shape. This recipe never fails, if followed carefully.

CUP CAKE

1 cup butter or oleo
2 cups sugar
3 eggs
4 cups sifted flour
1 cup milk
2 heaping teaspoons baking powder

SPICE CAKE

1 cup butter
1½ cups sugar
3½ cups flour
½ cup milk
5 eggs
1 teaspoon cinnamon
½ teaspoon cloves
½ teaspoon lemon essence
2 teaspoons baking powder

Proceed as with any other cake. Bake in layers in a moderate oven, and spread between the layers a marshmallow filling (below).

MARSHMALLOW FILLING

1½ cups sugar
   Whites of 2 eggs
18 marshmallows

Put the sugar to boil with enough water to make it melt properly, beat the whites and when sugar mixture is boiled enough to string when a spoon of it is poured slowly, add to the beaten whites, beat 1 minute, then put in 10 marshmallows, 1 teaspoon vanilla, beat until it begins to thicken, spread on the cake layers, and decorate the top layer with 7 or 8 whole marshmallows.

BANBURY TARTS

Roll pie crust to ⅛ inch thickness and cut in 3-inch squares. Mix together ¾ cup chopped raising, ¾ cup chopped dates, ¼ cup chopped nuts, 1 cup light brown sugar, 1 tablespoon flour, 1 egg, juice and grated rind of 1 lemon, and put a heaping teaspoon of the mixture on each square and fold over diagonally to form a triangle. Moisten the edges with a piece of ice, and use a fork to press the edges together. Bake in hot oven for about 20 minutes until brown.

NO-EGG GINGER BREAD

1½ cup New Orleans syrup or
   molasses
1 cup lard or oleo
1½ cups sugar
2 cups or 1 pound raisins
2½ cups water
2 teaspoons cinnamon
2 teaspoons ginger
1 teaspoon cloves
1 teaspoon salt
¼ teaspoon soda
2 heaping teaspoons baking powder

Enough sifted flour to make consistency of any other cake dough. Thick enough to put in pans with spoon, and too thick to pour.

Put water in pot on stove, wash raisins and put them in the water. Cook slowly until water comes to a boil. Have lard, syrup, sugar, spices, salt in deep bowl, pour in water and raisins, stir and mix well. Let cool for 15 minutes, add soda, baking powder and sifted flour. Bake in slow oven in flat pans or muffin rings.

CHOCOLATE BUTTER ICING

$1^1/_2$ tablespoons butter
2 cups confectioner's sugar
$1^1/_2$ square unsweetened chocolate, melted
4/5 tablespoons hot milk or cream

Cream the butter; add sugar gradually, add chocolate and milk or cream, using just enough to make right consistency to spread thickly.

CARAMEL CAKE FILLING

Set to boil 1 cup sugar, $^1/_3$ cup of milk and 1 tablespoon butter. Put another cup of sugar in hot iron skillet, and stir constantly until there are no lumps and the mixture has become a decided brown, then pour the first mixture, which has boiled a minute or two, into the skillet, remove from fire, scrape all that has stuck to the spoon into the skillet again, and stir and beat until it begins to get a little thick. Flavor with vanilla and spread hot between the cake layers.

CARAMEL SAUCE

2 cups granulated sugar
3 cups boiling water

Melt sugar in saucepan and heat, stirring constantly until golden brown; add boiling water. Cook 3 minutes.

SOFT GINGER CAKE

5 eggs
1 cup butter or oleo
1 cup sugar
1 cup New Orleans molasses or syrup
1 cup milk
$3^1/_2$ cups sifted flour
1 teaspoon each of ginger, cinnamon, cloves, salt
2 teaspoons baking powder

Beat eggs, sugar, butter until light, beat whites separately, mix in last after adding other ingredients, add baking powder, bake in large square tin pan in moderate oven, and cut in large squares and serve hot.

ECONOMICAL COOKIES

1 cup lard, lard substitute, or butter
$2^1/_2$ cups sugar
3 eggs
1 teaspoon salt
3 teaspoons baking powder
1 teaspoon lemon essence
3 teaspoons cinnamon
$^3/_4$ cup milk

Mix lard, sugar and eggs, salt and cinnamon, essence together until well mixed, add milk, and enough sifted flour to enable you to roll out cookies on biscuit board, and cut any desired shape, cook in moderate oven, and put away in tin box – they will keep for weeks.

PECAN CAKE

6 eggs
1¹/₂ cups sugar
1 heaping tablespoon flour
4 cups pecans chopped fine
1 teaspoon baking powder

Beat egg yolks ten minutes, add slowly the sugar, then put in nuts, flour and baking powder, then the stiffly beaten whites. Cook in two layers and use whipped cream to put together, or bake in 1 shallow pan, cut into inch squares and serve with whipped cream.

NUT COOKIES

¹/₂ cup butter or oleo
1¹/₂ cups sugar
2 eggs
3¹/₂ cups sifted flour
¹/₂ cup milk
1 cup chopped pecans
1 cup chopped citron
1 cup currants
2 teaspoons baking powder
   Cinnamon and lemon essence

Proceed as with other cookies, roll thin, bake carefully and as soon as done, before removing from pan, dust with powdered sugar.

CHOCOLATE NUT COOKIES

Proceed exactly as with recipe for nut cookies, but add 3 heaping tablespoons chocolate or cocoa. Bake carefully.

SOUTHERN TROPICAL CAKE
First Mystery Cake

¹/₂ cup shortening
1¹/₄ cups sugar
2 eggs
1 cup milk
2¹/₂ cups flour
4 teaspoons Royal baking powder
¹/₄ teaspoon salt
1 teaspoon cinnamon
1 teaspoon nutmeg

Cream shortening; add sugar slowly and beaten eggs; mix well. Add flour sifted with baking powder, salt and spices alternately with milk to first mixture. Pour ²/₃ of batter in 2 greased layer tins and to remaining third, add 1 tablespoon cocoa mixed with 1 tablespoon boiling water. Use this for middle layer. Bake in moderate oven at 375° F. about 20 minutes. Put Mocha Icing between layers and on top of cake.

MOCHA ICING AND FILLING

3 tablespoons butter
3 cups confectioner's sugar
5 tablespoons cocoa
5 tablespoons strong cold coffee
1 teaspoon vanilla extract

Cream butter: add sugar and cocoa very slowly, beating until light and fluffy. Add coffee and vanilla slowly, a few drops at a time, making soft enough to spread.

MISSISSIPPI RIVER STAGE PLANKS

(New Orleans Ginger Bread)

2   cups New Orleans molasses or cane syrup
$^1/_2$ cup sugar
1   cup oleo
3   teaspoons ground cinnamon
1   teaspoon ground cloves
1   teaspoon ground ginger
1   teaspoon salt
$^1/_2$ cup boiling water

If syrup or molasses is the least bit sour, use half teaspoon baking soda in the boiling water, and use 2 teaspoons baking powder.

Mix ingredients listed above, then sift in and mix with as much flour as you require to make a dough that can be moulded by the hands into flat "stage planks" about 6 inches long and 3 inches wide, and about half an inch thick. Set on greased pans 2 inches apart, so when they spread they will not touch each other. Bake in slow oven and look at them every few minutes, as anything that contains syrup or molasses is apt to burn very quickly. These will keep for a week or two if kept in a tin box.

GOLD CAKE

$1^1/_2$ cups sugar
3   cups sifted flour
$^1/_2$ cup butter or oleo
   Yolks of 8 eggs
$^1/_2$ cup of milk
2   teaspoons baking powder
   Essence of some sort, lemon, vanilla

CHOCOLATE DOUGHNUTS

2   eggs
1   cup sugar
2   squares chocolate
3   cups flour
1   teaspoon vanilla
4   teaspoons baking powder
$1^1/_2$ teaspoons salt
$^3/_4$ cup milk
$^2/_3$ cup nutmeats (optional)
   Grated rind $^1/_2$ orange

Beat eggs and sugar with spoon, add melted chocolate. Sift dry ingredients, add alternately with milk. Stir in nuts, rind and vanilla. Roll, cut and fry in deep fat 360-370° F. Roll in sugar if desired. These make a delicious dessert if served with a spoonful of whipped cream in center of each.

MERINGUES

   whites of 3 eggs
$1^1/_4$ cups granulated sugar
3   teaspoons Royal baking powder
$^1/_4$ teaspoon vanilla extract

Beat whites of eggs until stiff; add gradually $^2/_3$ of sugar and continue beating until mixture holds shape; fold in remaining sugar sifted with baking powder; add vanilla. Drop by spoonsful on unglazed paper and bake in slow oven at 250° F. for 30 minutes. Increase heat to 300° F. and bake 30 minutes longer.

1 cup nuts, cut fine, or 1 cup grated cocoanut may be folded into mixture before baking.

MUFFINS

4 cups flour, measured before sifting
2³/₄ cups milk, lukewarm
4 tablespoons sugar
1 teaspoon salt
1 heaping tablespoon melted butter
2 egg whites beaten separately
2 heaping teaspoons baking powder

Add beaten whites of eggs last, and bake in fairly hot oven. A half teaspoon of vanilla extract in my opinion improves the taste of the muffins.

BRAN MUFFINS

2 tablespoons butter
1 cup milk, either sweet or sour
1 egg
3 tablespoons sugar
1 cup bran
3 teaspoons baking powder
1 cup flour

Bake in moderate oven and serve hot. Makes 12 muffins.

COCOROONS

1 cup sugar
1 cup grated coconut
2 cups corn flakes
2 egg whites, stiffly beaten
¹/₄ teaspoon almond extract

Fold sugar into stiffly beaten egg whites. Folk corn flakes and coconut into mixture; gradually add extract. Drop from teaspoon on greased tin. Bake in moderate oven. Makes 3 dozen.

PECAN NUT-CAKE
(For Afternoon Tea)

1 cup butter, oleo
2 cups sugar
1 cup milk
5 eggs
5 cups sifted flour
2 teaspoons vanilla essence
2 heaping teaspoons baking powder
8 cups pecans, chopped fine

Make as you would any other cake, and at the last, put in chopped pecans, stir well, and bake in round cake pans, in slow oven. This cake should be iced and kept at least a week before it is eaten.

BROWNIES

2 eggs
1 cup sugar
2¹/₂ squares unsweetened chocolate
¹/₃ cup shortening
¹/₂ cup flour
¹/₂ teaspoon Royal baking powder
¹/₈ teaspoon salt
¹/₂ teaspoon vanilla extract
1 cup nut meats, chopped not too fine

Beat eggs until thick and frothy; beat in sugar. Melt chocolate and shortening together over hot water. Add to first mixture. Add flour sifted with baking powder and salt. Add vanilla and nuts. Spread thinly in greased shallow pan and bake in moderate oven at 325° F. for 30 minutes. Cut into 2-inch squares.
They may be iced if desired.

FRUIT CAKE

1 *pound butter*
1 *pound sugar*
1 *tablespoon flour*
10 *eggs*
1 *pound currants*
1 *pound raisins*
1 *pound citron*
1 *nutmeg*
1¹/₂ *teaspoon cloves*
2 *teaspoons cinnamon*
2 *teaspoons allspice*
1 *spoon soda dissolved in 1 cup molasses*
   juice and rind of 1 lemon
1 *orange*
1 *glass sherry (optional)*
1 *glass whiskey (optional)*
1 *pound pecans*
1 *pound mixed nuts*
1 *pound dates*
1 *pound dried figs*

Cream together butter and sugar. Add eggs one at the time, then add the spices, then sifted flour.

2nd dissolve soda in molasses, then pour in pastry.

3rd mix all fruits together and flour, whiskey and sherry, or fruit juices as a substitute.

These quantities make 4 nice size cakes.

Line each cake pan with heavy greased brown paper and cook very slowly at about 275° F.

TIPSY CAKE

1 large sponge cake, baked in tube cake pan. Soak in 2 cups any preferred wine, white wine, claret or port. 2 cups will suffice. Fill hole and top of cake with whipped cream and stud cream with whole pecans and red and green cherries.

CHOCOLATE ROLL

Beat 2 egg yolks; add 1 cup sugar slowly and 4 tablespoons cold water. Sift 1 cup flour with 1¹/₂ level teaspoons Royal baking powder and ¹/₂ teaspoon salt, and add alternately with 2 beaten egg whites. Spread very thinly on long greased pan. Bake in moderate oven about 15 minutes. Turn out on damp cloth sprinkled with powdered sugar – trim hard edges; spread with filling and roll in cloth while warm. When cool remove to plate, and sprinkle with powdered sugar. For Filling – Scald ³/₄ cup milk with 1¹/₂ squares melted unsweetened chocolate. Thicken with ¹/₄ cup flour mixed with ¹/₄ cup cold milk; add 1 tablespoon butter. Beat ¹/₂ cup sugar, 1 egg and ¹/₄ teaspoon salt together and add. Cook over hot water until smooth and thick. Add ¹/₂ teaspoon vanilla and spread. Jelly filling may be substituted for chocolate.

BAKED CUP CUSTARD

4 eggs
1/2 cup sugar
1/4 teaspoon salt
1 teaspoon vanilla extract
1 quart milk

Beat eggs, sugar, salt and vanilla together; scald milk and add slowly, stirring constantly. Put into baking or small pyrex molds; place in pan of water in slow oven at 300° F. and bake about 40 minutes. Test with knife which will come out clean when custard is baked.

For Caramel Custard, add to eggs 4 tablespoons Caramel Sauce.

A teaspoon of whiskey may be added to each cup before serving.

WHITE ICING

1 1/2 cups confectioner's sugar
2 tablespoons hot milk
1/2 tablespoon butter
1/2 teaspoon flavoring

Add butter to hot milk: add sugar slowly to make right consistency to spread: add flavoring. Spread on cake.

COLORED ICINGS

Pink Icing – add 1 tablespoon strawberry or other fruit juice.

Yellow Icing – add 1 teaspoon egg yolk and flavor with orange rind and 1 teaspoon lemon juice.

BOILED ICING

2 1/4 heaping cups sugar
3/4 cups water
2 tablespoons white corn syrup
beaten whites of 2 eggs
1/2 teaspoon extract

Put sugar and water into saucepan and boil until a thread forms, then pour slowly into beaten whites. Beat until stiff enough to spread on cake.

CHOCOLATE ICING

Add one cup cocoa or 2 squares to above icing while hot, beat well and spread on cake.

VANILLA CREAM FILLING

1/2 cup sugar
2 tablespoons cornstarch
1/8 teaspoon salt
2 eggs
1 cup scalded milk
2 teaspoons butter
1 teaspoon vanilla extract

Mix sugar, cornstarch, salt and beaten eggs; pour on gradually scalded milk; add butter; cook in double boiler until thick and smooth, stirring constantly; add flavoring and cool.

POUND CAKE

1 pound butter or oleo
1 pound flour
1 pound sugar
12 eggs
2 heaping teaspoons baking powder

Beat butter or oleo, whichever you are using, together with the sugar to a cream, add yellows of eggs, sifted flour a little at a time; then beaten whites and baking powder. Bake in loaf tins or in regular round cake pan, with hollow tube up the middle in moderate oven, for about 40 minutes – allow to cool in pan, then ice with cooked icing.

MEASURED POUND CAKE

8 eggs
2 cups butter
3 cups granulated or powdered sugar
4 cups sifted flour
1/2 teaspoon almond extract
2 heaping teaspoons baking powder

Proceed as with other pound cake, and bake in moderate oven about 40 minutes. This cake compares favorably with the weighed pound cake. Sometimes it is not convenient to weigh out a cake, so this recipe is a nice one for such emergencies.

WINE CAKES

Use recipe for pound cake, bake in large muffin rings. Half an hour before you are ready to serve these, pour 1/2 cup port or sherry wine over the cakes, top with teaspoonful whipped cream and 1 red cherry. Sometimes sparkling burgundy is preferred.

HASTY APPLE CAKE

6 medium-sized apples

Slice in bowl and sprinkle with 1/2 cup sugar, 1 teaspoon cinnamon and 4 small pieces of butter about 1/2 teaspoon each. Make a batter of:

1 cup flour
1/2 cup sugar
1/2 cup milk
2 eggs
1 tablespoon butter
1 teaspoon baking powder

Pour batter over apples which have been placed in baking pan. Bake in moderate oven for about 30 minutes. Serve either hot or cold with whipped cream, custard or sweet wine sauce, recipe for which you will find with recipe for pudding.

CHOCOLATE COOKIES

3 eggs
2 squares unsweetened chocolate
1/2 cup butter
1 cup sugar
1 cup flour
1 teaspoon vanilla extract
1 cup chopped English walnuts
2 level teaspoons vanilla

DATE CAKE

1½ cups chopped pecans
1 cup chopped dates
1 cup sugar
3 eggs beaten together before
    adding to sugar
1 cup flour
½ teaspoon baking powder

Mix part of flour with nuts and dates. Add remainder to other ingredients.

Bake in slow oven about 45 minutes. Serve with ice cream or tea or coffee.

DROP COOKIES

½ cup butter
¾ cup sugar
2 eggs
1½ cups flour
1 teaspoon almond extract
2 teaspoons baking powder

Proceed by cake method, beat well. Drop cookies 2 inches apart on greased tins and bake in hot ovens.

SUNSHINE DROP COOKIES

½ cup butter
½ cup sugar
1 egg, beaten until velvety
¾ cup flour, sifted twice
½ teaspoon vanilla

After beating well drop batter from a spoon size of a marble on a greased pan. Bake in moderate oven.

CAKE FOR PARTIES

½ cup butter or oleo
1 cup sugar
½ cup cane syrup
½ cup milk
½ cup cocoa
3 eggs
2 cups sifted flour
1 cup each chopped dates, raising,
    walnuts or pecans

Bake in very slow oven in shallow greased tin pans, turn out when cold. Dust with powdered sugar, cut in small squares and serve with ice cream or beverages. These are delicious with Creole coffee.

ROCKS

1½ cups sugar
3 cups flour
1 cup butter
⅓ cup water
1 cup raisins
1 cup chopped nuts
3 eggs
½ teaspoon each cinnamon and
    nutmeg
½ teaspoon soda

Cream the butter and the sugar. Add eggs then add the flour, cinnamon and soda after sifting together with the water (or milk) alternately. Add chopped nuts and raisins. Drop from teaspoon on greased tin and bake in moderate oven. Should make sixty.

FRENCH PETTICOAT COOKIES

2 cups butter
4 level cups flour
2 tablespoons milk
  grated rind of 1 lemon
1 cup sugar
1 heaping teaspoon baking powder

Cream butter and sugar, then add flour and baking powder that have been sifted several times, then milk and the grated lemon rind, then roll. Cut into triangles and bake in quick oven, and sprinkle with powdered sugar when baked.

When Mary Stuart left France to claim her Scottish Throne, her attendants brought back with them the recipe for these little cookies. The French called them "petits gateaux tailes," the Scotch translated this as "petticoattails."

JELLY ROLL

1 cup sugar, no more, no less
3 eggs, beaten separately
1 teaspoon baking powder
1 pinch salt
1 cup sifted flour

Use sponge cake method in mixing. Bake in square greased pan ³/₄ inch thick. If more dough than this is put in pan the cake will split in rolling. Take out of pan immediately it is done, spread with jelly and roll. Sprinkle with reddened sugar, roll a clean dish towel or napkin around it. Slice with very sharp knife when cold.

OATMEAL COOKIES

2¹/₄ cups raw oatmeal, the "quick" kind
1 cup raisins
³/₄ cup butter
1¹/₂ cups sugar
2¹/₄ cups sifted flour
3 teaspoons baking powder
2 eggs
1 heaping teaspoon cinnamon
1 scant teaspoon cloves
1 teaspoon allspice
³/₄ cup milk

Drop on greased pans and bake in moderate oven.

MINCEMEAT CAKE

1 cup shortening
2¹/₂ cups sugar
4 eggs, beaten separately
1¹/₂ cups mincemeat
4 cups flour
4 teaspoons baking powder
¹/₂ teaspoon salt
1 cup milk
¹/₂ teaspoon cinnamon
¹/₄ teaspoon allspice
¹/₂ teaspoon nutmeg
1 cup chopped nuts

Method: Cream shortening and sugar, add egg yolks and beat well. Sift flour with all other dry ingredients over the mincemeat and add alternately with the milk to the creamed mixture. Add nuts and fold in beaten egg whites. Bake in loaf, layers or ring mold in 350° F. oven. If made in layers, bake 45 minutes. Put together with orange icing.

WHITE FRUIT CAKE NO. I

1 *pound sugar*
1 *pound flour, sifted twice*
$^1/_2$ *pound butter*
  Whites of 12 eggs
2 *pounds chopped almonds or pecans*
1 *pound citron, chopped fine*
1 *teaspoon salt*
2 *heaping teaspoons baking powder*
1 *teaspoon almond extract*

Proceed as with any other white cake, and bake in large pan with hole up middle. When cold, remove carefully from pan, ice with pale-green icing, decorate with whole nuts, and keep for a day or two before using.

WHITE FRUIT CAKE NO. 2

$1^1/_2$ *cups sugar*
1 *cup butter*
  Whites of 10 eggs
4 *cups flour sifted*
$^1/_2$ *teaspoon soda*
1 *teaspoon baking powder*
1 *tablespoon lemon juice*
$^1/_2$ *pound candied pineapple*
1 *pound citron*
$^3/_4$ *pound candied cherries*
$1^1/_2$ *pounds raisins*
1 *pound chopped nuts*

Cream butter and sugar together, add alternately stiffly beaten whites and flour, then different fruits and nuts, add lemon juice, soda and baking powder, and put to bake in cake or bread pans in moderate ovens. Bake for about an hour and a half.

PLANTATION PUFF CAKE
(2 Cakes)

Take 2 thick layer cakes made from recipe of Old Fashioned Sponge Cake.

Take out of layer tin in which they have been baked, and place on outside of pan, upside down. Spread layer of chopped pecans $^1/_4$ inch thick on top of each layer, and spread on each cake a meringue made with:

3 *egg whites*
$1^1/_2$ *cups sugar*
$^1/_2$ *teaspoon almond extract*

Beat egg whites 5 minutes, then add about every 2 minutes a teaspoon of sugar, beating hard. Spread this meringue on each cake and bake very slowly with very low flame. Meringue should take 20 minutes to brown.

BRIDE'S CAKE

$^3/_4$ *pound butter*
1 *pound sugar*
1 *pound flour*
$^1/_2$ *cup milk*
  Whites of 17 eggs
1 *teaspoon salt*
2 *heaping teaspoons baking powder*
1 *teaspoon almond extract*

Cream the butter well, add sugar slowly spoon by spoon, beating slowly all the time. When the mixture is creamy enough, add the well beaten whites, a little at a time, alternating with a little flour until you have used both all up. Then add baking powder and extract, and bake in moderate oven.

CHOO PASTE

Bring ½ cup butter and 1 cup water to the boiling point, then add immediately 1 cup sifted flour. As soon as this mixture leaves sides of pot remove from fire, stir until cool, then add one at a time 3 eggs. When well beaten, bake in eclair shapes or small balls. This paste can be used for cream puffs and is extremely useful for French pastry combinations.

COCOONS

2¼ cups flour
  5 tablespoons powdered sugar
  1 cup nuts
¾ cup butter

Chop nuts and mix with flour and sugar. Melt butter and add to dry ingredients. Roll the dough into cocoons size and shape of your thumb and bake in slow oven about 45 minutes.

SHORT CAKE

1 pint flour, measured before sifting
2 heaping teaspoons baking powder
1 teaspoon salt
1 tablespoon sugar
1 cup milk
4 tablespoons lard

Mix, knead dough and spread it in two pie plates, bake in quick oven. Split open hot, and put in each, two cups fresh strawberries, raspberries or peaches.

CRACKER PUDDING

15 crackers soaked 1 hour in 1 pint
     boiling water
  2 cups sugar
½ cup butter or oleo
  4 eggs
  1 pint milk
  1 teaspoon vanilla essence

Save whites for meringue. Mix pudding as you would cake, adding essence and hot cracker mixture last. Bake ¾ of an hour in moderate oven.

Beat the 4 whites well, adding slowly 1½ cups sugar, spread on pudding and put back in slow oven until the meringue is brown. This pudding is better served cold. The crackers should have the boiling water poured over them, and then set aside to cool a little.

CHOCOLATE SQUARES

  2 squares Baker's chocolate
½ cup butter
  1 cup sugar
  2 eggs
½ cup flour
  1 cup chopped nuts
  1 teaspoon vanilla

Melt chocolate over hot water, add it to the creamed butter, sugar and eggs. Beat well for 10 minutes; add flour, extract and nuts. Turn into greased square pan preferably tin. Bake in moderate oven about 30 minutes. Turn out hot and cut immediately into squares.

BREAD PUDDING

4 *eggs*
1 *cup butter*
2 *cups sugar*
1 *quart milk*
1 *teaspoon salt*
2 *teaspoons baking powder*
1 *teaspoon nutmeg*
1 *teaspoon vanilla*
4 *cups toasted bread crumbs, rolled*
fine

(Toast your bread, roll it, then put the pieces left back in oven, and repeat until you have four cups.)

Beat butter and sugar together well. Add eggs, then bread crumbs, then milk and other ingredients. Serve hot.

Serve above pudding with custard made of:

1 *pint milk*
2 *eggs*
1 *tablespoon cornstarch*
1 *cup sugar*

Serve hot with pudding. Flavor with vanilla.

BATTER PUDDING

1 *pint milk*
1 *pint sifted flour*
1 *tablespoon sugar*
4 *eggs (don't beat separately)*
Pinch salt

Mix well, bake in moderate oven. Serve very hot with any desired sauce. Hard sauce (sugar and butter) is nice

ENGLISH PLUM PUDDING (BAKED)

1 *loaf bread preferably stale French*
1 *quart milk*
3 *cups sugar*
$^1/_2$ *pound butter or oleo*
2 *teaspoons nutmeg*
8 *eggs*
1 *pound raisins*
1 *pound currants*
3 *teaspoons baking powder*
1 *teaspoon lemon essence*

Put the milk to boil, break up the bread in small pieces. Pour milk over the bread and let stand for one hour. Cream butter and sugar, then add eggs, spice and raisins and currants. Then mix with bread, milk, and baking powder. Pour into buttered pan, bake in moderate oven for one hour. Do not serve until cold. Cut like cake. This will keep for two weeks.

PEACH COBBLER

Follow directions for peach pie but use a deep baking pan instead of a pie plate. Put $^1/_2$ cup whiskey in peaches just before you put them in crust. Serve with whiskey sauce given below.

1 *cup sugar*
$^1/_2$ *cup whiskey*
$^1/_4$ *teaspoon nutmeg*
2 *cups water, hot*

Caramel sugar in iron skillet, when light brown add hot water. Cook until caramel is melted. Pour into serving pitcher, add whiskey, spice, and serve hot with hot pie.

PERFECT MERINGUE

There is much variety to meringues but many complaints seem to group them into one – the fallen meringue. The several reasons for meringue falling are these: Too hot an oven: too little sugar: too little beating. A good meringue is given below:

> 4 egg whites
> 1³/₄ cups sugar
> Any preferred extract

Put whites in bowl and use wire egg beater. Beat until whites are nearly stiff, then add, every few minutes, a teaspoonful of sugar, beating well all the time, until the sugar is all used up. You will find the meringue quite stiff, and it can be heaped in fancy shapes on pies and cakes. Bake in very slow oven for 20 minutes until it browns slightly. You will find it hasn't lost its shape or fallen in the middle.

APPLE PIE

Use raw pie crust made by recipe in this book. Use five large apples to pie. Cut apples in thin slices, use sugar, half cup to every five apples. Put apples, sugar, half cup water in pot and boil slowly one-half hour. Cool thoroughly before putting in pie crust. Use criss-cross or solid top pie crust, as desired. Slightly cooked apples make much better pies than raw.

APPLE DUMPLING

Use recipe for biscuits, cut 8 large apples in quarters, add ¹/₂ cup water, 2 cups sugar and stew for half hour. Allow to cool, then roll dough in round pieces larger than saucer, put spoonful stewed apples, dash cinnamon, a little butter in middle of round dough, fold up tight and place smooth side up in pudding pan, until full. Bake in hot oven.

Grease pan with lard.

SAUCE FOR DUMPLINGS

Cores and peelings of applies used for dumplings. Place on fire with 2 quarts water, 1 cup sugar, and boil slowly 1¹/₂ hours. Strain, boil again, dissolve ¹/₂ cup flour and thicken sauce. Pour this over dumplings as you serve them.

OLD-FASHIONED MOLASSES PIE

> 1 pint open kettle molasses
> 2 tablespoons flour
> 1 tablespoon sugar
> ¹/₄ teaspoon nutmeg
> 1 tablespoon butter
> 3 eggs
> 1 teaspoon, level, soda

Beat all well and turn into raw crusts and bake for 30 minutes in moderate oven.

SOUTHERN CREAM PIE

¹/₂ cup sugar
1¹/₂ cups pie cherries
2 cups cherry juice
2 packages cherry gelatin
1 cup cold water
6 green cherries
1 cup whipped cream
1 baked pie shell
Whipped cream for garnish

Bring sugar, cherries and juice to boil. Strain over cherry gelatin, stir until dissolved, add cold water, chill. Pour a little of mixture into bottom of ring mold, arrange drained cherries and a few green cherries in cluster design. Pour in one inch of gelatin mixture and chill almost set. Beat remaining gelatin with rotary beater, add cherries and whipped cream, pour over clear gelatin. Chill until set. Unmold into large baked pie shell. Fill center with whipped cream.

OLD-FASHIONED CREAM PIE

1 pint milk
2 eggs
2 tablespoons cornstarch
1 cup sugar
A little salt, vanilla essence

Beat egg yolks up with sugar, add milk, put in double boiler to cook, when very hot, add cornstarch dissolved in 2 tablespoons water. Have ready 2 cooked pans of pie-crust, beat whites of eggs well, adding when stiff, sugar ¹/₂ cup – put the cream in pie-crust, spread meringue on top, and in very slow oven about 20 minutes until meringue is brown. Serve cold.

BAKED CRUST FOR ONE-CRUST PIE

1¹/₄ cups sifted flour
¹/₂ teaspoon salt
cup shortening
2-3 tablespoons cold water (about)

Sift flour and salt, add half the shortening, cutting it in with pastry blender or two knives until mixture looks mealy. Add rest of shortening, continue cutting until particles are size of navy bean. Sprinkle water, 1 tablespoon at a time, over mixture. Work mixture lightly together with fork, until moistened and in lumps. Use just enough water to moisten. Press particles together into a ball, drop on floured board, roll dough lightly to ¹/₈ inch thickness and about three inches larger than pan. Sprinkle ¹/₂ teaspoon flour over inside of 9-inch pan, place dough in pan, let stand 5 minutes to allow for shrinkage. Trim ¹/₂ inch larger than pie pan, then flute. Chill. Bake in very hot oven, 450° F., 15 minutes.

WASHINGTON PIE

¹/₃ cup butter
2 eggs
1 teaspoon vanilla
³/₄ cup sugar
1¹/₂ cups cake flour
¹/₂ cup milk
3 teaspoons baking powder

Cream butter and sugar, add eggs, beat hard. Sift flour and baking powder 3 times, add alternately with milk, add vanilla. Bake in 2 layer cake pans 20 minutes. Put together with custard.

TWO CRUST PASTRY

2¹/₂ cups sifted flour
³/₄ cup shortening
1 teaspoon salt
5 tablespoons cold water (about)

Sift flour and salt, add half the shortening, blending it with fork or two knives until mealy. Add rest of shortening, mixing until particles are size of navy bean. Sprinkle water, 1 tablespoon at a time, over mixture, adding just enough to moisten. Press dampened particles together into a ball. Roll lightly ¹/₈ inch thick on floured board. Make lower crust 2¹/₂ inches larger than pie pan. Fit dough into pan, patting pastry with ball of dough. Trim crust even with edge of plate, moisten edge, fill pie, adjust top crust. Fold top crust under lower crust, seal edges with tines of fork.

PECAN PIE

3 eggs
1 cup sugar
1 cup Louisiana syrup
1 cup chopped pecans
1 tablespoon butter
1 teaspoon vanilla extract
1 cup pecan halves

Cream butter, sugar, eggs, add syrup, vanilla and chopped nuts, turn into pie pans lined with raw pie crust, place the pecan halves in symmetrical design on top of pie mixture, and bake in moderate oven. The little lumber town out of Orleans seems to be the original home of pecan pie. Signs all over Slidell advertise the pecan pie and many New Orleanians drive out to buy them during the season.

PEACH PIE

Scald, skin and peel 12 large peaches. Cut into thin slices, mix well with 1¹/₂ cups sugar. Put in saucepan on stove and cook for 15 minutes after it begins to boil. Remove from fire and set to cool, then pour into three pie pans lined with raw pie crust, place criss-cross strips on top and bake in hot oven. Remember in handling pie crust to have it very cold and to use as little flour as possible in rolling it out. The recipe given in this book cannot fail if these directions are followed. There is no magic used in the making of good pie crust.

BERRY PIE

3 cups canned or fresh berries,
* drained*
1 cup fruit juice
* Sugar (if required)*
3 tablespoons quick-cooking tapioca

Combine fruit, juice, sugar and tapioca, let stand while making crust. Line a 9-inch pie pan with dough, pour in fruit and juice, adjust top crust, seal edge of pie. Bake in hot 450° F. oven, 30 to 40 minutes.

SWEET POTATO PIE

Take 1 quart boiled mashed potatoes, add 1 quart milk, 4 eggs, yolks and whites, 1 teaspoon salt, ¹/₂ teaspoon nutmeg, 1 teaspoon cinnamon, and sugar enough to sweeten. Bake in 4 raw pie crusts until solid in the middle.

COCOANUT PIE

This method of cooking cocoanut pie seems to belong to New Orleans and its vicinity.

4 *eggs*
4 *cups grated cocoanut*
1¹/₂ *cups sugar*
3 *cups milk*
   Pinch of salt and teaspoon vanilla essence

Use whole eggs. Beat them well, add sugar, milk, cocoanut, salt and essence. Have ready tin pie plates lined with raw pie crust. Pour mixture in, set in hot oven to cook about 20 minutes. When crust is brown and middle of pie seems solid, the pie is done. Serve either hot or cold. The recipe for pie crust will be found on page 71.

MINCE PIE

1 *cup canned mincemeat*
1 *cup chopped apple*
2 *tablespoons sugar*
2 *tablespoons whiskey or grape juice*

Bake in hot oven with double or criss-cross top crust, and sprinkle or sift powdered sugar on top soon as done.

CREOLE CREAM PIE

Use recipe for Jelly Roll. Bake in one deep layer cake pan in moderate oven at 350° F. about 30 minutes. When cool, split and put layers together with Vanilla Cream and cover top with powdered sugar.

RAISIN PIE

1 *pound seeded raisins*
3 *pie-pans water*
1¹/₂ *cups sugar*
³/₄ *cup cornstarch*
1 *teaspoon each of cinnamon, lemon extract*

Put water and raisins to boil, then stir 5 minutes. Add spice and extract. When cool, put in raw crust, criss-cross top crust. Bake in hot oven. 3 pies.

SOUTHERN DREAM PIE

3 *cups graham cracker crumbs*
1 *tablespoon sugar*
³/₄ *cup melted butter*

Combine and press ²/₃ of above mixture into pie shell, saving ¹/₃ for top of pie. Any pie filling desired may be used.

FLUFFY PIE

1 *cup sugar*
6 *teaspoons cornstarch*
   dash salt
1 *small can crushed pineapple*
1 *cup water*
2 *teaspoons lemon juice*
2 *egg whites*
³/₄ *cup nut meats chopped fine*

Mix together the sugar, cornstarch, salt, pineapple and water. Cook in double boiler about 20 minutes. When cold add the lemon juice and fold in the stiffly beaten egg whites. Fill in baked pie shell. This pie may be covered with whipped cream or chopped nuts or both. Serve ice cold.

LEMON OR ORANGE CUSTARD PIE

2/3 cup sugar
1/2 cup flour
1 1/2 cups milk
1 cup orange juice
1 teaspoon grated orange or lemon rind
2 eggs
1 tablespoon butter
4 tablespoons sugar

Into top of double boiler put sugar, flour and salt to taste, slowly add milk, stirring well; add orange rind and juice and cook until mixture is thickened. Add butter and pour into unbaked crumb crust. Make meringue of remaining egg whites and 4 tablespoons sugar, spread over pie and sprinkle reserved crumbs over. Bake in oven until meringue is light brown.

CUSTARD PIE

1 pint milk
3 eggs
1 teaspoon flour
1/2 cup sugar

Line pie pans with raw crust and pour raw custard and bake in moderate oven until custard is solid. Flavor with 1 teaspoon vanilla.

≋≋ ≋≋ ≋≋ ≋≋ ≋≋ ≋≋ ≋≋ ≋

Remember that ginger bread or any cake containing syrup or molasses burns easily, and should be baked in a very low oven. If you want your griddle cakes or waffles to brown easily, add 2 teaspoons of cane syrup to the batter.

RED CHERRY PIE FILLING

1 can sour red pitted cherries
1 1/2 cups sugar
2 heaping teaspoons cornstarch

Take liquid from can, put in pot with sugar, boil, add cornstarch mixed with 1 cup water, add cherries, 1 teaspoon almond extract, cool and put in raw pie crusts with criss-cross top. Bake in hot oven.

INDIVIDUAL PIES

Use patty pans, or turn your muffin rings upside down, fit pieces of pie crust (see recipe) around as many as you wish, and bake upside down in hot oven. Detach carefully, set to cool and fill with any pie filling. This is a change from the usual pie. This may also be used as patty shells for chicken, oysters, etc.

LEMON LUSH DELIGHT
(Refrigerate Overnight)

1 1/2 cups flour, 1 1/2 sticks butter (melted), 1 cup chopped pecans. Mix together and put into 9x13 pan. Bake 1/2 hour at 350° F. Cream one 8-ounce package Philadelphia cream cheese, 1 cup powdered sugar, 4 ounces Cool Whip or whipped cream. Spread on cooled crust. Mix 1 large size instant lemon pudding (Jello) and 1 tablespoon Galliano (optional). Pour over cream cheese mixture. Then another 4 ounces Cool Whip or whipped cream. Sprinkle with pecans.

CARAMEL ICE CREAM

3 eggs
3 cups sugar
3 quarts milk
1 quart cream
3 teaspoons vanilla extract
   pinch salt
$^1/_2$ cup cornstarch

Pour cream off 3 quarts milk and mix with quart of whipping cream and set in refrigerator, put the rest of milk in double boiler on low fire. Beat yolks to creamy lightness with 1$^1/_2$ cups sugar, mix with warm milk in double boiler. Add cornstarch as in any other custard, stir until thick, turn off fire. Caramel the remaining 1$^1/_2$ cups sugar in hot iron skillet and add to custard. When cool, add cream and vanilla, freeze in regulation freezer pack, and serve several hours later, if you want it at its best.

BANANA ICE CREAM

1   envelope gelatin
12 ripe bananas
2   cups sugar
1   quart milk
1   pint whipping cream

It is not necessary to use cornstarch in this cream. Gelatin is preferred. Soak 1 envelope of gelatin in $^1/_2$ cup cold water. Heat one cup milk, add to gelatin and mix with rest of milk and cream. Slice bananas in very thin round slices, mix with sugar and put all together and freeze immediately.

MAPLE PARFAIT

4 eggs
1 cup maple syrup
1 teaspoon gelatin
1 pint whipping cream
1 teaspoon vanilla

Beat yolks and syrup together and cook in double boiler. Cool on ice and add whipped cream and stiffly beaten whites and gelatin, which has been dissolved in 1 tablespoon cold water. Freeze and pack for 3 hours.

HARD SAUCE

$^1/_2$ cup butter
1$^1/_2$ cups sugar

Cream your butter, add sugar, a teaspoon every few minutes, beating all the time. If made carefully, should be pure white. Season with vanilla and serve on any hot pudding. Brandy may be added.

STRAWBERRY ICE CREAM

1   quart strawberries, very ripe
1   quart milk
1   pint whipping cream
2$^1/_2$ cups sugar
$^1/_4$ cup cornstarch

Mash ripe berries well with fork, mix with sugar. Thicken milk as in recipe for peach ice cream, with cornstarch and mix ingredients and freeze.

TUTTI FRUITTI ICE CREAM

1 cup nuts, chopped very fine
1 quart milk
1 pint whipping cream
2 cups sugar
1 cup red candied cherries, cut small
6 macaroons, mashed fine
1 teaspoon vanilla extract
1 tablespoon strawberry preserve
1/4 teaspoon almond extract
1 envelope gelatin
1/2 cup green candied cherries, cut up

Proceed with gelatin as in banana ice cream, then mix milk, cream and all other ingredients together and freeze. Serve with chopped nuts and thin slices of citron topping each parfait glass.

PEACH ICE CREAM

1/4 cup cornstarch
1 quart milk
1 pint whipping cream
9 large ripe peaches
1 1/2 cups sugar
vanilla extract

Plunge the ripe peaches into boiling water for one minute, prick with fork and peel, cut into very thin slices and mix with sugar. Pour cream off of milk, put remainder into double boiler, bring to boil, add cornstarch. Set to cool, mix with peaches and cream, add vanilla and freeze in regulation freezer.

BISCUIT TORTONI

1 pint whipping cream
4 eggs beaten separately
1 cup chopped maraschino cherries
1 cup chopped pecans

Beat whites slightly, add whipping cream, add yellows to whipped cream, then nuts and cherries. Freeze immediately.

AMBROSIA

6 ripe bananas
6 oranges
1 grated cocoanut
1 cup sugar

Cut oranges into small thin slices, cut bananas into thin round slices, add sugar mix, then spread grated cocoanut on top. Keep cold and serve. This makes a delicious and wholesome dessert.
Bananas may be left out if desired.

LEMON SHERBET

juice of 3 lemons
1 1/2 cups sugar
1 quart milk

Mix juice and sugar, stirring constantly while slowly adding very cold milk. If added too rapidly, mixture will curdle. However, this does not affect quality. Freeze and serve.

For Orange or Pineapple Sherbet use 2 cups strained fruit juice and 1 tablespoon lemon juice: reduce milk to 3 cups.

VANILLA ICE CREAM

6 egg whites
2 cups sugar
2 tablespoons gelatin, 1 cup water
1/2 cup water
1 quart cream
   Vanilla essence

Boil sugar and water together long enough for mixture to make hard ball when dropped into cup of cold water. Pour slowly into well beaten whites of eggs. Add gelatin, which has soaked in cup of water for 30 minutes. Beat well until cool, add cream, vanilla and freeze immediately. This makes a delicious cream.

HOT LIQUID SAUCE

1 cup of water
1 cup of milk
1/2 cup sugar

Boil water, milk and sugar together and stir in heaping table-spoon flour, dissolved in cold water. Cook till thick and season with vanilla, or add 1 cup whiskey.

ORANGE WATER ICE

   juice of 6 oranges
2 teaspoons orange extract
   juice of 1 lemon
1 quart water
2 cups powdered sugar
1/2 cup cream

Mix all ingredients together; strain and freeze.

PRUNE PUFF

4 egg whites
1/4 teaspoon salt
1/2 cup powdered sugar
1 cup prune pulp
1 teaspoon vanilla

Add salt to egg whites and then beat until stiff. Now add sugar very slowly, then the prune pulp (made from prunes cooked, seeded and chopped), then add vanilla. Put in Pyrex or baking dish into a slow 325° oven for 10 or 15 minutes. Serve with a topping of whipped cream, and a dab of crushed pecans or nuts. Serve iced cold.

CHARLOTTE ROUSSE

1 quart milk
6 eggs
2 teaspoons vanilla
2 cups sugar
   Pinch salt
2 envelopes Knox's gelatin

Soak gelatin in 1 cup water for half-hour. Make custard of yolks of eggs, milk and sugar, cook in double boiler. Have arranged in deep bowl, 12 lady fingers, or 12 slices of sponge cake. Mix custard with gelatin, beat whites of eggs to stiff froth, mix with hot custard, add 2 teaspoons vanilla, pour over cake in bowl, and set on ice for at least three hours. This is delicious frozen in refrigerator. If it is to be frozen, use graniteware to freeze in.

STRAWBERRY FREEZE

1 *can Pet milk*
¹/₂ lemon
2 *bottles strawberry pop*

To the can of Pet milk add lemon and whip, sweeten to taste, and add strawberry pop, and mix thoroughly. White of beaten egg may be added, if so desired, but not necessary.

STRAWBERRY MOUSSE

1 *box strawberries*
1 *cup sugar*
1 *tablespoon granulated gelatin*
2 *tablespoons cold water*
3 *tablespoons boiling water*
1 *quart cream*

Wash and hull berries, sprinkle with sugar and let stand one hour; mash and rub through fine sieve; add gelatin soaked in cold water and dissolved in boiling water. Set in pan of ice water and stir until it begins to thicken; fold in whipped cream and freeze. Raspberries or peaches or shredded pineapple may be used instead of strawberries.

≈≈ ≈≈ ≈≈ ≈≈ ≈≈ ≈≈ ≈≈ ≈≈ ≈≈

Time is saved in chopping raisins or marshmallows if scissors are used in cutting them up.

BREAD PUDDING

5-6 *slices French bread*
4 *tablespoons sugar*
3¹/₂ *cups milk*
4 *eggs, separated*
    Raisins and diced apples
¹/₂ *stick butter*
1 *tablespoon vanilla*

Break bread into ovenproof pyrex. Add a little milk to soften. Beat sugar and egg yolks. Add milk, vanilla, salt and pour over bread. Add raisins and apples and butter. Place in pan of water and bake at 300° F. about 50 minutes. Make meringue with egg whites adding 2 tablespoons sugar for each egg white. Return to 350° F. oven until brown.

BLACK OR STRAWBERRY SHERBET

2 quarts strawberries or blackberries from which juice has been mashed and squeezed, sweeten to taste, and freeze. Whipped cream or the stiffly beaten white of an egg, may be folded in before freezing.

FROZEN CREAM CHEESE

1 *quart milk*
2 *cream cheese*
¹/₂ *pint cream (whipping)*
2 *teaspoons vanilla*

Take cream cheese and mash through a sieve, add milk, and sweeten to taste. Add the whipped cream and whip, or mix thoroughly. Add vanilla extract and freeze.

CREAM FREEZE

1 cup milk
18 marshmallows
1 teaspoon vanilla extract
1 cup cream, whipped to honey
   consistency
1 cup ground nuts

Cook milk and marshmallows in double boiler until dissolved. Cool, add cream, extract and nuts; mix, and freeze in tray of mechanical refrigerator.

ORANGE MOUSSE

1 pint whipping cream
$^{1}/_{2}$ cup sugar
1 teaspoon gelatin
$^{1}/_{4}$ cup water
$^{3}/_{4}$ cup orange juice
$1^{1}/_{2}$ oranges
2 egg whites stiffly beaten

Whip cream, add sugar, flavor with orange and juice. Melt gelatin that has been soaked in $^{1}/_{4}$ cup of water. When cool, add to cream the stiffly beaten egg whites. Line mold with orange that has been separated. Pour in cream. Freeze.

ICE CREAM PISTACHIO

$^{1}/_{2}$ cup chopped pistachio nuts
1 teaspoon almond extract
   few drops green coloring
$^{1}/_{4}$ teaspoon salt
1 cup sugar
4 cups cream

Mix all the ingredients and freeze.

FRESH STRAWBERRY ICE CREAM

$^{1}/_{2}$ cup sugar
1 pint strawberries
3 tablespoons tapioca
2 cups milk, scalded
$^{1}/_{4}$ teaspoon salt
6 tablespoons light corn syrup
2 tablespoons sugar (XXXX)
2 eggs
1 cup whipping cream

Add $^{1}/_{2}$ cup sugar to strawberries and crush well. Let stand $^{1}/_{2}$ hour. Proceed as for Vanilla Ice Cream folding in strawberries just before adding whipped cream. Makes 1 quart.

FRUIT COCKTAIL SHERBET

1 can fruit cocktail
1 lemon
$^{1}/_{2}$ cup sugar

Mix together fruit cocktail, juice of lemon and crushed pineapple, sweeten thoroughly, freeze in electric refrigerator. Serve and garnish with cherries.

CUSTARD ICE CREAM

2 cups milk
2 tablespoons cornstarch
²/₃ cup sugar
2 egg yolks
1 teaspoonful vanilla
½ pint whipping cream

Scald the milk in double boiler. Add the cornstarch and sugar well mixed and cook for 10 minutes or until thick, stirring constantly. Put into baking dish slightly beaten egg yolks, return to double boiler and cook 3 to 5 minutes longer, or until custard thickens. Cool. Add vanilla and fold in whipped cream.

Crushed sweetened fresh strawberries or peaches may be added after it begins to freeze.

CREOLE ICE CREAM

1 quart cream
1 cup sugar
1 tablespoon vanilla extract

Scald half pint of cream; add sugar and stir until dissolved. Cool and add remainder of cream and vanilla. Freeze.

CHOCOLATE ICE CREAM

Use recipe for Creole Ice Cream. Melt 2 squares unsweetened chocolate, add sugar and stir; add the hot cream slowly to make a smooth paste. Combine with remaining cream and freeze.

LOUISIANA SUGAR HOUSE

CHOCOLATE FUDGE

3 cups sugar
3 heaping tablespoons cocoa
1/4 teaspoon salt
3 tablespoons Karo syrup (crystal white)
1 cup milk
1/2 bar butter
2 teaspoons vanilla
1 1/2 cups nuts – pecans or peanuts

Put sugar, cocoa and salt in pot, and mix thoroughly then add Karo syrup and mix, put to cook until it forms a soft lump in cold water, then remove from fire and add butter. When almost cold or cool enough to hold hand underneath the pot, add vanilla and beat until creamy. Add nuts and pour into a dish that has been buttered, cut in squares when cold.

You may use peanut butter instead of nuts which makes a very delicious and creamy fudge.

PECAN PRALINES

1 1/4 cups white sugar
3/4 cup brown sugar
1/2 stick butter
1/2 cup milk
1 teaspoon vanilla
2 cups pecans

Cook sugar and milk to soft-ball stage, add butter. When melted, take from fire and beat until it begins to thicken. Add nuts and vanilla, and drop a teaspoonful at a time on oiled or buttered paper.

COCOANUT PRALINES

2 cups sugar
4 cups fresh grated cocoanut
3/4 cups water
1 tablespoon butter (level)

Boil sugar and water and butter together until mixture forms ball in cup of cold water, then put in the grated cocoanut, boil slowly until mixture forms ball in cold water. Have greased platters ready, put spoonfuls a few inches apart, allow to cool, then lift carefully by running a thin knife under each praline. Some people prefer a few drops of vanilla in the mixture. If pink pralines are desired, a few drops of red coloring is added.

CREOLE PECAN PRALINES

2 cups sugar
3/4 cup water
1/2 tablespoon vinegar
4 cups pecan halves

Put to boil sugar, water and vinegar until syrup makes a soft ball when dropped into cup of cold water. Put in pecans, cook until syrup forms a hard ball in cup of cold water. Have ready large platter or pans greased with butter. Drop a large spoonful of the mixture about six inches apart, and let them cool. When hard and cold, run knife under each praline, and put on plate.

GLACÉ NUTS AND FRUITS

1 cup sugar
1 cup Karo syrup
1/3 cup water

Boil until syrup brittles instantly in ice water. Keep hot in double boiler. Dip nuts and fruits in one at a time. Use an icepick to take out, lay on well buttered plate. They harden immediately.

PECAN NOUGAT

2 cups sugar
2 cups pecans, chopped fine
1 teaspoon butter

Use iron skillet. Put sugar and butter into skillet, melt slowly stirring continually, until the sugar is a dark caramel.
Put pecans in immediately, mix and pour into buttered tin, cut immediately. This confection is delicious, but requires speed, skill and planning to be a success.

WALNUT CANDY

2 cups brown sugar
1 tablespoon butter
1 cup walnuts
1 cup milk

Boil the sugar and milk until a little dropped in cold water forms a soft ball. Add butter. Remove from fire and beat until it begins to thicken, add nuts and pour into buttered pan. Cut in squares.

MOLASSES CANDY
(Candi Tire a la Melasse)

Louisiana is rightly the home of Molasses Candy, for it was right here, in this old city, in the environments of which sugar was first raised in the United States, and molasses, sweet and healthgiving, was first given to the world, that Molasses Candy, or "Candi Tire," as the Creoles call it, first had birth. "Candi Tire" parties, or Molasses Candy Pullings, were among the pleasurable incidents of life among the early New Orleans belles and beaux. Take

1 quart of Louisiana molasses
1 tablespoon of butter
1 pound of granulated sugar
2 tablespoons of vinegar
1/2 teaspoonful of soda
  the juice of 1 lemon
1 teaspoon banana extract

Boil the sugar until it becomes quite thick when dropped into water. Add the molasses and the vinegar and butter. Boil till it hardens when dropped into cold water. Then stir in a small half teaspoonful of bicarbonate soda, and pour into buttered tins, and as soon as it begins to cool sufficiently pull till white. Moisten the hands while pulling with ice water or butter. The sticks may be single, twisted, braided or flattened, according to taste.
While pulling add banana extract by drops.

PEANUT BRITTLE

Put cup of granulated sugar in iron skillet and stir until it syrups, being very careful not to burn. Push back from flame, and quickly stir in cup of peanuts which have been shelled, skinned and heated in oven, adding teaspoon butter and tiny pinch of soda. Turn at once as thinly as possible onto greased slab or buttered platter. When cold, break in pieces.

DATE LOAF CANDY

2¹/₂ cups of sugar
1 cup of sweet milk

Cook until same almost hardens, in cup with cold water. Add piece of butter size of walnut, one package of seeded and chopped dates and one cup of chopped pecans. Beat until nearly hard. Roll in damp cloth and when cool unroll and cut in slices.

DATE KISSES

2 egg whites
1 cup powdered sugar
1 cup chopped nuts
1 cup chopped dates

Beat whites very stiff, add sugar, dates and nuts. Drop on greased tins and bake slowly, watching very closely.

CANDIED ORANGE OR LEMON PEEL

Peel of 4 oranges or 6 lemons
1 cup sugar
¹/₂ cup water

Cut the peel and cover with cold water. Boil slowly until tender. Drain, cool enough to handle, and remove with spoon white lining of peel. Cut into thin strips. Boil cup sugar and half cup water together until they form a heavy thread. Add peel and cook 5 minutes. Drain and roll in sugar. Use the syrup for flavoring icings.

PEANUT CANDY

2 cups granulated sugar
¹/₄ teaspoon salt
³/₄ cup chopped peanuts

Heat the peanuts and salt together; put sugar in an iron pan, place over a low flame and stir constantly until the sugar is changed to a light brown syrup. Add the chopped peanuts and salt, stirring them in as quickly as possible. Pour immediately into a hot buttered pan, divide into squares with a chopping knife.

STUFFED DATES

Remove stone from dates, place one-half pecan meat inside of date. Press together firm and roll in sugar.

CHOCOLATE CARAMELS

2 cups molasses
1 cup cream or milk
4 tablespoons butter
1 cup brown sugar
1/4 pound of sweetened chocolate
1 teaspoonful vanilla flavoring

Put all ingredients but vanilla, into kettle. Boil until it hardens when tested in cold water. Add vanilla and turn into flat greased tins. When nearly cold, cut into small squares.

PECAN CARAMEL

3 cups granulated sugar
1 cup milk
2 tablespoons butter
2 cups chopped pecans
1 1/2 cups sugar

Boil the 3 cups of sugar with milk. Melt the 1 1/2 cups of sugar in an iron skillet to caramel. When the sugar and milk mixture forms a soft ball when dropped in cold water (to test) add the caramel, nuts and butter. Take off and beat until creamy.
Pour on buttered dish. When cold, cut into squares.

If you intend to shell a large quantity of pecans for cakes, candies, or salting, put them in boiling water for 10 minutes. Turn fire out after. You will find they will crack easily without breaking the nut.

DATE LOAF

2 cups pecans
3 cups sugar
1 cup milk
1 pound dates

Mix all together and cook until it leaves the side of pot, then when taken from fire add 2 cups of pecans. Put in wet napkin and roll. Cut in slices when cold and sprinkle with powdered sugar.

DIVINITY FUDGE

2 cups sugar
1 egg white
1 teaspoon vanilla or almond extract
1/2 cup walnut or pecan meats or both
1/2 cup corn syrup Karo (crystal)
1/2 cup water

Cook sugar, syrup and water stirring occasionally, until it forms a thread when dropped from spoon. Add syrup to the stiffly beaten egg white pouring slowly and beating constantly.
When it begins to thicken, add chopped nuts, spread on buttered dish and cut into squares when set. Chopped cherries and pineapple are also delicious when added with nuts.

PERSIAN FUDGE

1 *can condensed milk*
1 *cup sugar*
2 *tablespoons butter*
1 *cup chopped pecans*
1/2 *cup chopped raisins*
1 *tablespoon vanilla or your*
   favorite extract

Put sugar and condensed milk into heavy pot, and cook slowly stirring constantly. When the milk and sugar are melted and browned, add butter and extract, nuts, etc. Spread on buttered dish, cut in squares.

SALTED ALMONDS

Peel two pounds almonds, put in boiling water for three minutes, drain through colander, and immediately slip skins off. Put one heaping table-spoon butter or oleo in iron skillet, with almonds, two level tablespoons salt. Cook over moderate heat, stirring constantly, until almonds are brown as desired.

"DAGO" POPCORN

2 *eggs*
1/2 *teaspoon salt*
   flour

Beat eggs and add salt and flour, working in until you can either cut into small thin squares, or roll into small balls size of small marble.
Drop into hot deep fat. Cook quickly. Put on brown paper to dry, and pour over syrup made as for icing.

SYRUP FOR ICING

1 *cup sugar*
1/4 *cup water*
1 *teaspoon butter*
1 *teaspoon vanilla*

Cook water and sugar till it threads. Add butter and extract and pour over any popcorn. Delicious.

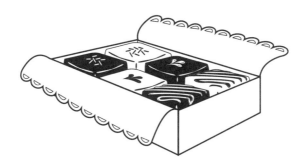

MEMO

HOUSEHOLD HINTS

≋ ≋

To clean furniture, wash with warm water and Ivory soap. Dry and rub with equal quantities of spirits of turpentine and sweet oil, wipe dry and rub with soft flannel cloth.

≋ ≋ ≋ ≋

To destroy ants, place a small lump of camphor in spot infested with ants. This will destroy them. Also a mixture of boiling water and salt poured into tunnel in nests is efficacious.

≋ ≋ ≋ ≋

To stop a cut bleeding, use equal portions of salt and flour mixed.

≋ ≋ ≋ ≋

To remove onion odor from hands, rub hands with celery.

≋ ≋ ≋ ≋

For burns, apply equal parts of white of egg and olive oil. If applied at once, it will not blister.

≋ ≋ ≋ ≋

An antidote for iodine poisoning, or to remove iodine stains: Take internally or apply at once starch water.

≋ ≋ ≋ ≋

To crisp celery or green vegetables: Add 1 tablespoon vinegar to pan of water and let stand.

≋ ≋ ≋ ≋

Should sink drains get choked: Pour into sink 1/4 pound Coperas dissolved in 2 quarts boiling water. Repeat if necessary.

≋ ≋ ≋ ≋

If meat is rubbed over with a little powdered borax, it will keep perfectly sweet and fresh for several days in the hottest or dampest weather without destroying the flavor of the meat.

HOUSEHOLD HINTS

≋≋ ≋≋ ≋≋ ≋≋ ≋≋ ≋≋ ≋≋ ≋≋ ≋≋ ≋≋ ≋≋ ≋≋ ≋≋ ≋≋ ≋≋ ≋≋ ≋≋ ≋≋

Should meats or vegetables burn slightly, a slice of stale bread placed in pot and covered will help remove burnt taste.

≋≋ ≋≋ ≋≋ ≋≋

Olives when opened should be kept uncovered in refrigerator.

≋≋ ≋≋ ≋≋ ≋≋

Pesky pin feathers are easily removed from fowls by rubbing melted paraffin lightly over them.

≋≋ ≋≋ ≋≋ ≋≋

Baking Soda is "a must" in your medicine chest or first aid kit. It has eight very helpful uses in your Red Cross First Aid Text Book.

1. On all burns, apply as soft paste on cotton pad.

2. As emetic in poison cases (except Alkali poisons).

3. Hives.

4. Hiccups.

5. Poison Ivy.

6. Insect bites.

7. Marine life irritation.

8. As gargle for colds.

INDEX

EGGS AND ENTREES

MEAT AND POULTRY

VEGETABLES

SALADS AND COCKTAILS

HOT BREADS, ROLLS

CAKES, COOKIES, FROSTINGS, SWEET SAUCES

PIES

ICE CREAM AND SHERBETS

CANDIES

Tony Frederick
3722 Tamara Street
Abbeville, Louisiana 70510

Please send me _____ copies of **Famous Old New Orleans Recipes** Cookbook at $9.95 each. Please add $3.05 per copy for postage and handling. Louisiana residents please add Louisiana sales tax.

Enclosed is my check or money order for   _____

                                    TOTAL   _____

Make checks payable to **Tony Frederick**

Name_____

Address _____

City _____ State_____ Zip_____

Tony Frederick
3722 Tamara Street
Abbeville, Louisiana 70510

Please send me _____ copies of **Famous Old New Orleans Recipes** Cookbook at $9.95 each. Please add $3.05 per copy for postage and handling. Louisiana residents please add Louisiana sales tax.

Enclosed is my check or money order for   _____

                                    TOTAL   _____

Make checks payable to **Tony Frederick**

Name_____

Address _____

City _____ State_____ Zip_____